WHAT MAKES AN ALCOHOLIC DIFFERENT FROM A NON-ALCOHOLIC?

The physiology of the alcoholic—not psychological makeup or cultural background—is the chief determining factor, a conclusion that has had major impact on the way we perceive and understand alcoholics today.

Under the Influence removes the stigma of guilt from alcoholism. It explains how enzymes, hormones, genes and brain chemistry work together to create this abnormal, addictive reaction. Moreover, it suggests changes that can be made in our social programs, our research and our medical profession so that alcoholism can finally be recognized for what it really is—a disease.

"I give *Under the Influence* to my patients when I first make the diagnosis of alcoholism. It's been very effective. A tremendous teaching tool, and one of the best books on the subject I know."
—Dr. Nicholas A. Pace, M.D.
Specialist, Internal Medicine

"I find Dr. Milam's concept absolutely extraordinary and very exciting."
—Mrs. Marty Mann, Founder-Consultant,
National Council on Alcoholism

"This is the one book to be left somewhere for the alcoholic to find and read."
—Toby Rice Drews
Author, *Getting Them Sober*

UNDER THE INFLUENCE

A Guide to the Myths and Realities of Alcoholism

James R. Milam, Ph.D., and Katherine Ketcham

BANTAM BOOKS

NEW YORK • TORONTO • LONDON • SYDNEY • AUCKLAND

UNDER THE INFLUENCE:
A GUIDE TO THE MYTHS AND REALITIES OF ALCOHOLISM
*A Bantam Book / published by arrangement with
Madrona Publishers, Inc.*

PUBLISHING HISTORY

*Madrona Publishers edition published October 1981
Bantam edition / December 1983*

ISBN 0-553-27487-2

Published simultaneously in the United States and Canada

PRINTED IN THE UNITED STATES OF AMERICA

OPM   40   39   38   37   36   35   34   33   32   31

Foreword

I am thrilled with this book. It meets a great need. I know that it will be understood and utilized so that millions of lives can be saved.

Under the Influence clearly points out that the accumulated evidence from all the life sciences positively indicates that physiology, not psychology, determines whether a drinker will become addicted to alcohol or not. The alcoholic's genes, enzymes, hormones, brain and other body chemistries work together to create his abnormal and unfortunate reaction to alcohol. This concept has not been and is not now understood or accepted even by the majority of alcoholism professionals, who seem committed to the misconception that alcoholism is, at least in part, caused by social, cultural, and psychological factors and is therefore treatable through mental health methods such as various psychotherapies and behavior modification techniques.

In 1970 James R. Milam wrote and self-published *The Emergent Comprehensive Concept of Alcoholism*. The book was enthusiastically welcomed by thousands of readers, both professionals and laypersons. Many of us said, "Here for the first time is someone who really knows what alcoholism is all about and who has finally put it down on paper." Fifty thousand copies of Milam's *Concept*, which was written in a relatively technical and clinical language, have been sold to date. This was accomplished without benefit of marketing, advertising, or the sponsorship of a publishing house. The demand for and acceptance of this new idea has indeed been phenomenal.

In Under the Influence, this original concept has been expanded, restated, and presented in a thoroughly understandable and fascinating explanation of alcoholism. It has been written with such clarity that many of the highly complex issues related to alcoholism become clear for the first time. Indeed, I feel this book is not only intended to be a textbook for professionals, clinicians, and academicians, but will also be welcomed and easily understood by the lay public. The authors have articulated ideas and truths which many of us have "known" or felt intuitively were underlying the disease alcoholism. For the first time, these ideas, concepts, and truths have been expressed with a validity based on research, documentation, and fifteen years of extensive clinical experience at Alcenas Hospital and elsewhere.

Thousands of alcoholics are seen every year by professionals—psychiatrists, psychologists, social workers, clergy, counselors, nurses, and doctors—yet, tragically, they are almost always misdiagnosed and often harmfully treated. It is my belief that alcoholism has suffered more malpractice out of ignorance than any other disease in recent times. Yet it is a disease that strikes our society so severely that, if unchecked, it could bring our nation to its knees.

It is my prayer and fervent hope that the concepts so clearly and boldly stated in *Under the Influence* have emerged at a time when they can be broadly recognized and accepted. They are truly ideas whose time has come. It is my further hope and prayer that the treatment approach described herein will be widely adopted as a basis for treatment of alcoholism in the future.

Under the Influence will aid and advance by light years the understanding of alcoholism and the recovery process. The labors of Milam and Ketcham in researching, documenting, and writing *Under the Influence* have placed us all in their debt. Let us hope that this book will spread light into darkness and bring us closer to a complete understanding of the disease alcoholism, and through this new understanding reach millions of our fellow men and women who today are suffering—and dying—because of society's ignorance.

MEL SCHULSTAD
Cofounder and past president of the
National Association of Alcoholism Counselors

Acknowledgments

We are especially grateful to Mrs. Dorris M. Hutchison, cofounder and for eleven years Executive Director of Alcenas Hospital. More than any other individual she is responsible for exploring and demonstrating the validity of this new approach to alcoholism treatment.

Special thanks go to Patrick Spencer, Fisher Howe, Elizabeth Howe, Kathe Monroe, and Bill Asbury for their advice and support.

Our greatest acknowledgment must always be a tribute to Alcoholics Anonymous, the inspiration and guiding force of the reform movement in alcoholism since 1935.

There are many anonymous human beings to whom this book refers only by pronouns. In the interest of stylistic simplicity, masculine pronouns generally have been used. The book, however, is dedicated to all who suffer from the disease of alcoholism, both men and women.

Contents

UNDER THE
INFLUENCE

1

Every Human Soul

Every human soul is worth saving; but . . . if a choice is to be made, drunkards are about the last class to be taken hold of. . . .

From "Drunkenness a Vice, Not a Disease,"
by J. E. Todd, 1882

Bob is 26 years old and a talented song writer. He says he drinks heavily for any number of reasons—when he is depressed because his work is not progressing well, elated because he finished a song, frightened about his future, or concerned about his financial problems.

When he drinks, he has problems. His car is scarred with dents and scratches from his erratic driving. He sometimes "forgets" what he did while he was drinking, and the next day he tries to piece together the night before. On one drunk, he broke his leg jumping over a fence. His wife takes a lot of abuse when Bob drinks. He hasn't hurt her badly, just slapped her around some. After a New Year's Eve party, Bob was driving, drunk, and his wife asked him to let her drive. Furious, he stopped the car, leaned across her, opened the door, and pushed her out. Then he sped away, leaving her stranded on the highway.

After these episodes, Bob feels guilty and ashamed and vows to cut back on his drinking. He begs his wife's forgiveness, and together they try to understand what bothers him when he is drinking and why he cannot just stop after a few drinks. Bob thinks the problem is psychological. He tells his wife that his career is difficult and demanding; the ups are euphoric, he explains, but the downs are devastating. Anyone would drink in this work, he tells her; it just comes with the territory. His wife blames the heavy drinking and violent behavior on his upbringing. His mother was a big drinker and set a bad example; furthermore, she never gave her kids any love or affection. Bob is just insecure, his wife insists. He needs understanding and tender loving care. She knows that he is a sensitive, loving man, and she believes she can be most helpful by supporting and helping him through the rough times.

Both Bob and his wife believe the drinking is just a symptom of some deep insecurity or emotional hangup. Once Bob becomes successful and their financial situation is secure, they believe he will have the confidence to work his problems out more rationally. "It is just a temporary problem," they agree.

Bob is an alcoholic. His wife, doctor, friends, and relatives do not know that he is addicted to alcohol. He does not know it either, although he is often afraid that something terrible is happening to him. He worries that he may have some kind of mental problem, although he struggles with these fears by himself, convinced that once he admits them they will be confirmed. He is deeply ashamed of himself and full of guilt about his inability to control his drinking and keep his promises to his wife.

What will happen to Bob? If he is like most of the 10 million alcoholics in the United States,* his children will be ashamed of him, his friends will shun him, his doctors will despair of helping him, and his wife will finally leave him. His personality will be gradually distorted, his talents and intelligence wasted, and his integrity and self-respect eroded. He will take tranquilizers and sedatives in an effort to combat his depression and anxiety. He will switch doctors, hoping to find one who can tell him what is wrong. He will see a psychiatrist and spend countless hours and thousands of dollars trying to dig up the roots of his unhappiness. He will be reprimanded by his boss, and eventually he will be fired.

Throughout it all, he will drink. He will try to stop drinking, and sometimes he will succeed. But after a week or a month, he will start again. He will shake, sweat, and feel sick to his stomach when he stops drinking. As he continues to drink, these withdrawal symptoms will get worse, and he will drink more, and more often, to relieve his pain.

As his disease progresses, his blood pressure will escalate, and his depression will increase. The drinking will not stop but instead will become more and more of a problem, causing difficulties at home, on the job, with the children. His heart, liver, and nervous system will begin to function less effectively. He will be hospitalized from time to time for various complications caused by his excessive drinking.

He will have numerous accidents—falling down the stairs or off a ladder, driving his car into a tree, overdosing on sleeping pills or tranquilizers—and one of these accidents may kill him. He may commit suicide.

---

*Most experts estimate the number of alcoholics in the United States around 10 million, but many suggest that the number may stretch as high as 20 million.

Or he may eventually die from "acute alcohol poisoning," cirrhosis of the liver, heart or respiratory failure, pneumonia, or infection.

Most alcoholics will die 10 to 12 years earlier than their nonalcoholic friends. Most will never receive treatment for their primary disease of alcoholism. Their death certificates will typically state "heart failure," "accident victim," "suicide," or "respiratory failure" as the cause of death. The chances are that no one—physician, social worker, family member, or alcoholic—will diagnose the cause of the problem as addiction to alcohol.

While thousands of alcoholics like Bob die every year, scientists, physicians, and professional alcoholism specialists argue endlessly about the nature of the disease that destroys them. The people involved in trying to understand alcoholism—and that includes psychologists, psychiatrists, physicians, nutritionists, biologists, neurophysiologists, biochemists, anthropologists, and sociologists—are sunk in a morass of conflict and confusion, admitting to prejudiced opinion, self-interest, and a deep distrust of others in the field. These professionals cannot agree about the causes of the disease, how it should be treated, or how it can be prevented.

The problem is deeper than a superficial disagreement among scholars. Violent feeling lurks here. Hatred, distrust, and prejudices abound. Profound insecurities and long-standing feuds smolder. Each scientist or research team appears to be working in a narrow compartment, oblivious of work conducted by others outside their special field. Scientists in the laboratory accuse the clinicians, who work directly with alcoholics, of ignoring scientific data and conforming to old-fashioned and out-dated treatment methods. Clinicians accuse the scientists of dismissing all first-hand experiences with alcoholics as "nonscientific" and therefore invalid. Government administrators chide the scientists for their

4

"intellectual arrogance," while the scientists accuse the bureaucrats of pandering to fads and special interests. Psychiatrists fret about being displaced from their positions as primary therapists and treatment personnel by a new wave of paraprofessionals specifically trained in alcoholism diagnosis and treatment.

These deep and painful schisms were dramatized at a recent conference which brought together eminent researchers and clinicians to discuss research priorities on alcohol.[1] The research priorities were put on the back burner, however, while the professionals spent three days attempting to sort out the confusions, hostilities, and deep divisions which plague the field. As one participant summarized the situation:

> . . . this topic is one of deep, immediate emotional cleavages fashioned through generations by a variety of traditional beliefs of moral, political, religious, educational, social class and other systems—cleavages which are carried by researchers and everybody else whether they like it or not.
>
> Quite apart from what general publics may think about alcohol researchers, it is hard to be unaware that representatives of one research discipline frequently feel that other disciplines dealing with alcohol-man-and-society are somewhat stupid on this topic.

Another prestigious researcher compared the alcoholism field to a chaotic collage created by children:

> [The field of alcoholism] reminds me of a large wall mural in a classroom, upon which the children worked for several years. . . . The mural did not have any central or unifying themes, save that it presented the opportunity for many contributors to add their personal ideograph.

5

Because of their confessed prejudices and self-interest, it should come as no surprise that these professionals are unable to pull the field out of its morass and invest it with new enthusiasm and energy. They have ceased to be part of the solution to the problem and instead have become part of the problem. "Clearly the current generation of alcohol researchers is too far gone," a participant concluded, "too steeped in our own disciplinary affiliations to be of much use; our shackles have become comfortable."

As long as the experts remain "comfortably shackled" to their own prejudices and self-interest, the layman will be confused and misinformed about alcoholism. The scope of this confusion and misunderstanding is truly astonishing, given the abundance of factual information already known about the disease. For example, alcoholism is known to be a true physiological disease which transforms its victims, leaving them with little or no control over their behavior. Yet the majority of people in this country—professionals and nonprofessionals alike—stubbornly cling to the belief that alcoholism is an emotional "weakness" and a moral evil capable of destroying society. Note such influential views as the following:

- Representative Samuel Devine (R-Ohio) in 1974 in explaining to the 2nd session of the 93rd Congress why he did not believe alcoholism is a disease: "My opinion is that it is a weakness, because otherwise we could attribute all our weaknesses to disease."
- Representative H. R. Gross (R-Iowa) on June 27, 1974, introducing an amendment to reduce the budget for the National Institute on Alcohol Abuse and Alcoholism (NIAAA): If the federal government provides funds for "those who let themselves become victims of booze," then it should also aid those addicted to gambling, nicotine, golf, and Southern grits, as well

as kleptomaniacs and "once virile men suffering from impotence brought about by women's liberation."

- Morris Chafetz, director of NIAAA, in addressing a special prevention task force on alcoholism, December 17, 1973: "I do not happen to believe that alcoholism is a disease." Instead, it is ". . . a symptom of a myriad of psychological and social problems."

- Representative Robert K. Dornan (R-California), as reported in the *Congressional Record*, October 25, 1979: "There is one major cause underlying alcohol abuse, drug abuse, and many other of the ills that afflict our society; it is an absence of self-discipline. This has broader implications than the statistics of premature death and disability would indicate. The social and economic disruption caused by such widespread self-abuse can undermine the strength of an entire society. A democratic society cannot survive and prosper without a virtuous people. And virtue is impossible without self-discipline."

- Columnist Jack Anderson, in a speech to the National Conference of Religious and Lay Leaders in November 1979: "The problem is real. There is something about morality that either makes a nation strong or saps its strength. Drunkenness corrodes society. . . . Alcohol and drug abuse is greater than a personal problem, although it is that. . . . Anything that degrades, despoils or debilitates human personality is evil. Anything that enlarges it, is good."[2]

A 1972 study of public attitudes toward various disabilities conducted by *Human Behavior* magazine found alcoholism and mental illness at the bottom of the list, rated "least acceptable." Ex-convicts, hunchbacks, dwarves, diabetics, amputees, heart patients, paraplegics, and epileptics were all considered more "acceptable" than alcoholics.[3] Clearly, this survey shows that most people continue to hold tight to the moralistic view that alcoholism is a shameful weakness, epitomized by the Skid

Road bum. Unlike the hunchback, who is the unlucky victim of fate, the ex-convict who has served his time and paid for his crimes, or the heart patient, diabetic, and epileptic, who are victims of diseases over which they have no control, the alcoholic is believed by most people to have chosen his fate. The diabetic or epileptic is a victim of his disability; the alcoholic is considered the cause of his.

In a 1979 survey sponsored by General Mills, 67 percent (or 2 out of 3) of 2,181 respondents felt that alcoholism is a sign of "personal emotional weakness"; 14 percent believed the disease had aspects of both a health problem and a personal emotional weakness; and only 19 percent considered alcoholism to be solely a health problem. Overall, when asked how serious they believed alcoholism to be, 46 percent replied "somewhat serious," 42 percent replied that heavy drinking is a "very serious threat to health," and 12 percent replied that it is "not a threat at all." Out of a list of thirty possible health threats, drinking ranked eleventh after industrial waste, pollution, marijuana, crash diets, cigarettes, diet pills, overweight, pesticides, tranquilizers, and cholesterol.[4]

In fact, alcoholism is ranked the number 2 killer in this country, behind cancer.* There are over 10 million alcoholics in the United States alone, and hundreds of thousands die every year of alcohol-related causes. Alcohol is involved in 60 percent of reported cases of child abuse and the majority of cases involving wife beating. Forty-one percent of the assaults, 39 percent of rapes, and 64 percent of criminal homicides involve alcohol. Between 35 and 64 percent of the drivers in fatal traffic accidents had been drinking. One quarter of the pedes-

---

*Since alcoholism is so often the undiagnosed cause of listed "causes" of death (e.g., heart or respiratory failure), many experts believe that alcoholism actually outranks cancer as the number 1 killer in the United States.

trians killed in 1979 were drinking. Up to 80 percent of suicides had been drinking.

The visible cost to the economy approaches a staggering $50 billion each year. Alcoholics fill up our prisons, mental institutions, hospitals, and welfare rolls. In terms of lost production, alcohol costs industry over $19 billion each year; health and medical costs run over $13 billion, motor vehicle losses over $5 billion, violent crime $3 billion, and fire at least $340 million. The hidden costs of undiagnosed and unrecognized alcoholism raise the costs even higher.[5]

The irony is cruel that the average man and woman consider the disease less of a threat than diet pills.

Alcoholism is tragically and fundamentally misunderstood. Every aspect of the disease is confused, distorted by myth and misconception, and colored by opinions which have no firm basis in fact. The roots of these myths are deeply buried in an ethical code of behavior that stretches back in time thousands of years. The Roman philosopher and lawyer Seneca (4 B.C.–A.D. 65) pronounced an opinion about drinkers and drunkenness that continues to mold public opinion: "Drunkenness is nothing but a condition of insanity purposely assumed."

Today, the alcoholic is generally considered to be a moral degenerate who chooses a life of abasement and, through lack of will power and maturity, allows himself to lose his job, his family, and his self-respect. The typical alcoholic, the myth informs us, is a person who would rather be drunk than sober, who lacks confidence and maturity, who is riddled with guilt and shame over past sins and misdeeds, yet lacks the strength of character to change his ways, and who has no guiding purpose or motivation in life. This myth is only one of many which rule the way we think about the disease and its victims.

The myths and misconceptions surrounding the

9

disease of alcoholism and its victims must be rooted out and replaced by already established facts. Only then will professionals cease their infighting and come to an agreement about the causes of the disease; only then will an understanding be reached about why alcoholics drink excessively and what must be done to help them overcome their disease. Only when the myths no longer cloud perception and shape opinion can alcoholics and their disease finally be understood.

A substantial body of scientific facts and information about alcoholism already exists—more than enough to guide research, intervention, and effective treatment. The problem is not a lack of knowledge, but the fact that this knowledge is scattered all over the landscape of the various life sciences. What is needed is not more isolated facts and information but a truly unifying scientific view of alcoholism. To be successful, such a concept must meet two primary criteria: (1) All hard data and facts must be respected and accommodated; (2) only those theories and beliefs that are compatible with the already established hard data and facts should be accommodated.

It is the primary purpose of this book to present just such a view of alcoholism. *Under the Influence* is a guide to the myths and realities of alcoholism. It offers— for the alcoholic and those who hope to understand and treat him—a clear explanation of a disease that has, until now, eluded explanation. This book looks at the substance—alcohol—that causes the disease and explains why this combination chemical, drug, and food is relatively harmless for some but addictive for others. It examines the causes of alcoholism and its gradual but inevitable progression from an early, hidden stage through the first noticeable signs of trouble and on to the catastrophic later stages. The alcoholic's symptoms are described and the question, "Why does he drink when drinking is destroying him," is clearly answered. The reader learns how to help the alcoholic into treatment and what kind of treatment the alcoholic must receive if he is to break his addiction and achieve a permanent, lasting sobriety.

Finally, the fundamental changes that must occur in social programs, government agencies, research, education and prevention efforts, the medical profession, and Alcoholics Anonymous are carefully outlined and explained. The very workings of our society in all these areas must shift and change focus if alcoholics are ever to receive the kind of help they deserve.

Separating myth from reality is not an easy task. Myth is, in fact, reality for many people; to suggest that another reality exists is to turn their world upside down. But if the truth about alcoholism is ever to be understood, the myths must be attacked and destroyed. Only facts can destroy myths; and facts are the backbone of this book.

The Myth and the Reality*

MYTH: *Alcohol is predominantly a sedative or depressant drug.*

REALITY: Alcohol's pharmacological effects change with the amount drunk. In small quantities, alcohol is a stimulant. In large quantities, alcohol acts as a sedative. In all amounts, however, alcohol provides a rich and potent source of calories and energy. (Chapter 2)

MYTH: *Alcohol has the same chemical and physiological effect on everyone who drinks.*

REALITY: Alcohol, like every other food we take into our bodies, affects different people in different ways. (Chapter 2)

---

*Chapter references are provided to help the reader find more in-depth information on these myths and realities.

MYTH: *Alcohol is an addictive drug, and anyone who drinks long and hard enough will become addicted.*

REALITY: Alcohol is a selectively addictive drug; it is addictive for only a minority of its users, namely, alcoholics. Most people can drink occasionally, daily, even heavily, without becoming addicted to alcohol. Others (alcoholics) will become addicted no matter how much they drink. (Chapter 2)

MYTH: *Alcohol is harmful and poisonous to the alcoholic.*

REALITY: Alcohol is a normalizing agent and the best medicine for the pain it creates, giving the alcoholic energy, stimulation, and relief from the pain of withdrawal. Its harmful and poisonous aftereffects are most evident when the alcoholic stops drinking. (Chapters 3 and 4)

MYTH: *Addiction to alcohol is often psychological*

REALITY: Addiction to alcohol is primarily physiological. Alcoholics become addicted because their bodies are physiologically incapable of processing alcohol normally. (Chapters 3 and 4)

MYTH: *People become alcoholics because they have psychological or emotional problems which they try to relieve by drinking.*

REALITY: Alcoholics have the same psychological and emotional problems as everyone else before they start drinking. These problems are aggravated, however, by their addiction to alcohol. Alcoholism undermines and weakens the alcoholic's ability to cope with the normal problems of living. Furthermore, the alcoholic's emotions become inflamed both when he drinks excessively and when he stops drinking. Thus, when he is drinking and when he is abstinent, he will feel angry, fearful, and depressed in exaggerated degrees. (Chapters 3 and 5)

MYTH: *All sorts of social problems—marriage problems, a death in the family, job stress—may cause alcoholism.*

REALITY: As with psychological and emotional problems, alcoholics experience all the social pressures everyone else does, but their ability to cope is undermined by the disease and the problems get worse. (Chapters 3, 4, and 5)

MYTH: *When the alcoholic is drinking, he reveals his true personality.*

REALITY: Alcohol's effect on the brain causes severe psychological and emotional distortions of the normal personality. Sobriety reveals the alcoholic's true personality. (Chapters 3 and 9)

MYTH: *The fact that alcoholics often continue to be depressed, anxious, irritable, and unhappy after they stop drinking is evidence that their disease is caused by psychological problems.*

REALITY: Alcoholics who continue to be depressed, anxious, irritable, and unhappy after they stop drinking are actually suffering from a phenomenon called "the protracted withdrawal syndrome." The physical damage caused by years of excessive drinking has not been completely reversed; they are, in fact, still sick and in need of more effective therapy. (Chapter 5)

MYTH: *If people would only drink responsibly, they would not become alcoholics.*

REALITY: Many responsible drinkers become alcoholics. Then, because it is the nature of the disease (*not* the person), they begin to drink irresponsibly. (Chapters 3 and 4)

MYTH: *An alcoholic has to want help to be helped.*
REALITY: Most drinking alcoholics do not want to be
helped. They are sick, unable to think rationally,
and incapable of giving up alcohol by themselves.
Most recovered alcoholics were forced into treatment against their will. Self-motivation usually occurs during treatment, not before. (Chapter 8)

MYTH: *Some alcoholics can learn to drink normally
and can continue to drink with no ill effects as long
as they limit the amount.*
REALITY: Alcoholics can never safely return to drinking because drinking in any amount will sooner or
later reactivate their addiction. (Chapter 9)

MYTH: *Psychotherapy can help many alcoholics achieve
sobriety through self-understanding.*
REALITY: Psychotherapy diverts attention from the
physical causes of the disease, compounds the
alcoholic's guilt and shame, and aggravates rather
than alleviates his problems. (Chapter 7 and 9)

MYTH: *Craving for alcohol can be offset by eating
high sugar foods.*
REALITY: Foods with a high sugar content will
increase the alcoholic's depression, irritability, and
tension and intensify his desire for a drink to
relieve these symptoms. (Chapter 9)

MYTH: *If alcoholics eat three balanced meals a day,
their nutritional problems will eventually correct
themselves.*
REALITY: Alcoholics' nutritional needs are only partially met by a balanced diet. They also need
vitamin and mineral supplements to correct any
deficiencies and to maintain nutritional balances.
(Chapter 9)

MYTH: *Tranquilizers and sedatives are sometimes useful in treating alcoholics.*

REALITY: Tranquilizers and sedatives are useful only during the acute withdrawal period. Beyond that, these substitute drugs are destructive and, in many cases, deadly for alcoholics. (Chapters 9 and 10)

2

Alcohol

As better knowledge and understanding of the actions of alcohol becomes available, more sensible attitudes regarding it are arising, [but] it is also interesting to observe how little the people wanted to learn about alcohol in a scientific way. They seem much to prefer their violently differing emotional fantasies about it.

Chauncey D. Leake, in a symposium
called "Alcoholism," 1957

Alcohol is an infinitely confusing substance. In small amounts it is an exhilarating stimulant. In larger amounts it acts as a sedative and as a toxic, or poisonous, agent. When taken in very large amounts over long periods of time, this combination chemical and drug can be damaging to cells, tissues, and organs. Yet alcohol is addictive for only a minority—an estimated 10 percent in the United States—of it users. For most drinkers alcohol is a relatively harmless social beverage.

To further the confusion, alcohol is the only drug which can also be classified as a food. Rich in calories and a potent source of energy for the body, alcohol is used by the cells to perform their complicated functions. Unlike most foods, however, alcohol contains negligible amounts of vitamins and minerals and contributes little or nothing to the cells' nutritional requirements. As a result, continual heavy drinking inevitably leads to malnutrition.

Perhaps alcohol's most surprising property is its ability to relieve the distress it creates in the first place. An alcoholic suffering from withdrawal has only one priority: alcohol. A malnourished alcoholic does not want food; he wants alcohol. Alcoholics drink because drinking makes them feel good. Only when they stop drinking do they experience the full effect of alcohol's disruptions in the body.

Understanding the disease alcoholism must begin with an understanding of the substance alcohol—a combination chemical, drug, and food capable of creating both extraordinary pleasure and extraordinary pain.

Alcohol the Chemical

What It Is

Ethyl alcohol or ethanol (hereafter called simply alcohol) is actually the excrement of yeast, a fungus with a ravenous appetite for sweets. When yeast encounters honey, fruits, berries, cereals, or potatoes, for example, it releases an enzyme which converts the sugar in these materials into carbon dioxide (CO_2) and alcohol (CH_3CH_2OH). This process is known as fermentation. The yeast then continues to feed on the sugar until it literally dies of acute alcohol intoxication— the very first victim of "drunkenness."

Because yeast expires when the alcohol concentration reaches 13 or 14 percent, natural fermentation stops at this point. In beer, which is made from barley, corn, rice, and other cereals, the fermentation process is artificially halted somewhere between 3 and 6 percent alcohol. Table wine contains between 10 and 14 percent alcohol, the limit of yeast's alcohol tolerance.

Distillation, which was discovered about A.D. 800

in Arabia, is the man-made process designed to take over where the vulnerable yeast fungus leaves off.* The distilled, or hard, liquors, including brandy, gin, whiskey, scotch, rye, bourbon, rum, and vodka, contain between 40 and 75 percent pure alcohol. Pure alcohol is also added to fortify wines such as port and sherry, boosting their percentage of alcohol to 18 or 20.

The percentage of alcohol in distilled liquors is commonly expressed in degrees of "proof" rather than as a percentage of pure alcohol. This measure developed from the seventeenth-century English custom of "proving" that an alcoholic drink was of sufficient strength by mixing it with gunpowder and attempting to ignite it. If the drink contained 49 percent alcohol by weight or 57 percent by volume, it could be ignited. Proof is approximately double the percentage of pure alcohol. A 100 proof whiskey is therefore 50 percent pure alcohol; an 86 proof whiskey is 43 percent alcohol.

Pure alcohol is a colorless, somewhat volatile liquid with a harsh, burning taste, which is widely used as a fuel and as a solvent for various fats, oils, and resins. This simple and unpalatable chemical is made to look, taste, and smell appetizing by combining it with water and various substances called congeners. Congeners make bourbon whiskey taste different from Scotch whiskey, distinguish one brand of beer from another, give wine its "nose" and sherry its golden glow.

Congeners include a wide variety of substances, many of which appear to have no business in a beverage designed for human consumption. Inorganic substances such as aluminum, lead, manganese, silicon, and zinc are frequently found in alcoholic beverages, as are glucose, fructose, acetic and lactic acids, carbon dioxide, small amounts of vitamins and minerals, salts, acids, ketones, esters, carbohydrates, and various other alcohols including propyl, butyl, amyl, hexyl, hyptyl, octyl, nonyl, decyl,

---

*"Alcohol" is derived from the Arabic "alkuhl," meaning essence.

methyl, and fusel oil. In minute or trace amounts, most congeners are harmless, but they have also proven toxic and even fatal for unsuspecting drinkers. Cobalt, for example, was once used to increase the foamy "head" in certain beers. Years went by before researchers finally linked the mineral with a rising cancer rate in beer drinkers.

How It Works

When human beings drink alcohol, it travels rapidly to the stomach, where approximately 20 percent immediately passes through the stomach walls into the blood stream. The remaining 80 percent is transferred from the stomach to the small intestine, where it is then absorbed into the blood stream.

The concentration of alcohol in the body is described by researchers in terms of the blood alcohol level (BAL), which is simply a measure of the percentage of alcohol in the blood. A .05 BAL, for example, indicates approximately 5 parts alcohol to 10,000 parts other blood components. When a person drinks more alcohol than his body can immediately eliminate—at the average rate of approximately one-half ounce per hour, the equivalent of 1 ounce of 100 proof whiskey or about 3 ounces of wine—alcohol accumulates in the blood stream, and the BAL rises. As the BAL rises, the drinker's behavior, thoughts, and emotions are increasingly affected, with severe disruptions in behavior occurring at high BALs. A person with a .10 BAL, for example, is considered legally "under the influence" in most states.

A number of factors can affect the rate at which the BAL rises and thus the rate at which behaviors are altered. Weight is one factor. The more the drinker weighs, the more water there is in the body to dilute the alcohol and therefore the lower the BAL. A 200-pound male might have an approximate .15 BAL after drinking eight cans of beer, whereas a 150-pound male, drinking at the same rate, might have a .20 BAL with the same intake. The higher BAL would, of course, make the

150-pound male act drunker. It is therefore the BAL and not the amount consumed which determines the effect on behavior.

Sex is another factor which affects the BAL. Females reach higher BALs faster because they have less water in their bodies and more adipose tissue (fat), which is not easily penetrated by alcohol. Hormones also affect the BAL. With the same intake of alcohol, women experience the highest BALs premenstrually and the lowest BALs on the first day of their menstrual cycle, fluctuations which are almost certainly caused by changing hormone levels.

Food or lack of it can alter the BAL. An empty stomach has no other foods with which to dilute alcohol and slow down its absorption into the blood stream. As a result, the BAL rises more rapidly in those who drink on an empty stomach. When there is food in the stomach, particularly high protein foods such as cheese, meat, and eggs, the absorption rate is slowed down.

The type of mixer also affects absorption. Water and fruit juices slow the process, while carbon dioxide speeds it up. The carbon dioxide in champagne and carbonated mixers such as Coca Cola, ginger ale, and quinine water rushes through the stomach and intestinal walls and into the blood stream, carrying alcohol along with it and creating a rapid rise in BAL.

The strength of the drink will also have a significant effect on absorption rates, with higher concentrations of alcohol resulting in more rapid absorption. Pure alcohol is generally absorbed faster than diluted alcohols such as 86 proof gins, which are, in turn, absorbed faster than wine or beer. An unusual effect may occur, however, in certain drinkers. Alcohol taken in concentrated amounts can irritate the stomach lining to the extent that it produces a sticky mucus which delays absorption. Furthermore, the pylorus valve which connects the stomach and small intestine may go into spasm in the presence of concentrated alcohol, trapping the alcohol in the stomach instead of passing it on to the small intestine where it would be more rapidly absorbed into the blood stream. As a result, the drinker who downs several straight shots of alcohol in an effort to get a quick high may actually experience a delayed effect.

Finally the temperature of the beverage affects its absorption, with warm alcohol being absorbed more rapidly than cold alcohol.

Once in the blood stream, alcohol is distributed throughout the body in simple diffusion. Its small and relatively simple molecular structure allows it to pass right through cell membranes and mix in the entire water content of the body. The brain, liver, heart, pancreas, lungs, kidneys, and every other organ and tissue system are infiltrated by alcohol within minutes after it passes into the blood stream.

Alcohol's immediate effect on the brain is most unusual. The brain is usually protected from chemicals and drugs by an electrical-chemical filter system known as "the blood/brain barrier," which makes sure that only very simple molecules such as those of oxygen and water can pass through. The simple molecular structure of alcohol allows it to penetrate this selective screen and gain easy access to the brain and its extension, the spinal cord.

Consequently, alcohol has immediate and profound effects on behavior. At low doses, alcohol stimulates the brain cells, and the drinker feels happy, talkative, energetic, and euphoric. After one or two drinks, the normal drinker may experience some improvement in thought and performance. As the BAL rises, however, the amount of alcohol in the brain also rises, and alcohol begins to disrupt the brain's electrical and chemical circuitry, causing complicated behavior changes.

With large amounts of alcohol surging through the brain's labyrinthine passageways, the central nervous system cells can no longer function normally. The brain malfunctions, and the major visible effect is a change in the drinker's psychological and emotional state. After several drinks, the normal drinker may begin to show signs of intoxication. He may become emotionally demonstrative, expressing great joy, sadness, or anger. He may also begin to show signs of motor incoordination, staggering slightly when he walks, knocking his drink over as he leaves the table, or slurring his words. If he continues to drink, his vision may blur, and his emotions, thoughts and judgment may become noticeably disordered.

When blood alcohol concentrations reach very high levels, the brain's control over the respiratory system may actually be paralyzed. A .30 BAL is the minimum level at which death can occur; at .40 the drinker may lapse into a coma. At .50 BAL, respiratory functions and heartbeat slow drastically, and at .60 most drinkers are dead.

The body, in the meantime, is doing its best to eliminate alcohol. Small amounts are eliminated in the urine, sweat, and breath, but the primary site of alcohol elimination is the liver, which is located behind the ribs on the right side of the body. This vital organ is responsible for numerous life-sustaining processes, including the control and elimination of drugs and chemicals which are toxic to the body's cells and the conversion of various nutritional substances into materials which can be used in the life processes of cells—processes such as eliminating wastes, making repairs, and creating new cells.

The process of elimination begins as soon as alcohol enters the liver. An enzyme called alcohol dehydrogenase (ADH) attacks the alcohol molecule, quickly removing two hydrogen atoms to create a new substance called acetaldehyde. Since acetaldehyde is a highly toxic agent which can produce nausea, rapid heart beat, dizziness, headache, and mental confusion if present in the body in large quantities,* the liver quickly initiates the second step in the elimination process. It employs another enzyme with a similar name, aldehyde dehydrogenase, to transform acetaldehyde into acetate. Acetate is then converted to carbon dioxide and water and eventually eliminated from the body. During these two steps in alcohol oxidation, a great deal of energy is released. In fact, with ordinary rates of alcohol metabolism, almost the entire energy needs of the liver can be satisfied. Most of the acetate is passed into the blood stream and oxidized to carbon dioxide and water in other organs. The energy produced in these reactions contributes to the energy needs of the entire body. In the alcoholic, up to two-thirds of the body's total energy needs may be satisfied by substituting alcohol for other foods. This explains why alcoholics often neglect eating for several weeks at a time.

The conversion of alcohol into acetaldehyde and acetate is an efficient process in most drinkers. The liver works at maximum efficiency, converting alcohol at the rate of approximately one-half ounce per hour, until all the alcohol in the body is broken down and its energy released to the cells. The liver is then able to return to its other duties.

If alcohol is present in the body in large amounts for long periods of time, however, the liver must work constantly to break it down and flush it out. The liver's preoccupation with alcohol results in the neglect of its other duties and, as a result, toxins accumulate and nutritional functions are disrupted. The health and vitality of the body's cells, tissues, and organs begin to suffer.

---

*The drug Antabuse, which is used with recovering alcoholics as a deterrent to drinking, blocks the liver's ability to eliminate acetaldehyde and causes an immediate and severe reaction. See chapter 10, pp. 162-166.

Alcohol the Drug

Alcohol is the most commonly used drug in the world, and yet even habitual users do not understand exactly how it affects them. When asked to describe alcohol's pharmacological properties, most people, including alcohol specialists, would reply "a sedative." When asked if alcohol is an addictive drug the majority of drinkers and nondrinkers would answer "yes."

Both answers are only partially true. Alcohol in large amounts is a sedative, but initially in small amounts, it is a true stimulant directly to nerve tissues. Furthermore, alcohol is an addictive drug only for the minority of its users who are physically susceptible.

Stimulant and Sedative

A shot of whiskey, a glass of wine, or a bottle of beer will trigger a variety of stimulating responses throughout the body. Numerous studies report that low doses of alcohol increase blood flow, accelerate heart rate, step up the conduction and transmission of nerve impulses, and excite simple spinal and brain stem reflexes. Performance on highly complex problem-solving tasks is improved with low doses of alcohol, memory and concentration are sharpened, and creative thinking is enhanced.[1]

Anyone who drinks can attest to these stimulating effects of low doses of alcohol. After a drink, or even a few sips, the average drinker feels warm and suffused with a sense of well-being. Ideas multiply, confidence increases, frustrations ease, and feelings of comradery, amusement, and contentment swell and grow. For most people, the world definitely seems a better place after a drink or two. Through simple conditioning or learning, even the anticipation of a drink can trigger some of these pleasant effects.

If it were not for these stimulating effects of alcohol, most people would soon lose interest in drinking. In fact, when alcohol's sedative effects begin to take over after several drinks, the pleasure and excitement of drinking are gradually cancelled out, and the average drinker simply stops drinking. A built-in deterrent to overdrinking seems to be working in most drinkers, somewhat like the natural deterrent to overeating which most people have, although the mechanism is different. The average person enjoys sweets, for example, and will eat a candy if it is offered. Some people will eat two or three, and a few will gobble down the whole box. Most people, however, will feel sick if they eat more than a small amount of concentrated sweets.

Likewise, the average drinker is unable comfortably to drink more than a few beers, a glass or two of wine, or several mixed drinks. The benefits of drinking are usually available only with low doses of alcohol, and when sedation begins to override the stimulation, the average drinker ceases drinking. Another deterrent is the toxic effect of several drinks in the normal drinker—the nausea, dizziness, sweating, and other unpleasant sensations.

The point at which alcohol's stimulating effects are overshadowed by the sedative and toxic effects varies from drinker to drinker. For some people, one drink is the limit. Others can drink four, five and more drinks and still experience alcohol's stimulating and euphoric effects. Alcoholics develop an increased physical resistance to alcohol's effects (called "tolerance"), and some can drink many times more than nonalcoholics while continuing to behave as if they were on their first few drinks.* Thus alcohol remains stimulating and pleasureable for alcoholics even after they have drunk amounts which would cause nonalcoholics acute discomfort.

---

*See chapter 4 for a discussion of tolerance.

For alcoholics as well as nonalcoholic drinkers, however, alcohol's stimulating effects will eventually be erased with continued drinking. After several drinks—again, depending on the initial tolerance of the drinker—the average person will begin to experience a slowing down in his mental and physical reactions. He may not be able to grasp the thread of a conversation; his reflexes will be somewhat delayed, his speech slurred, and his gait unsteady. As he continues to drink, the alcohol increasingly depresses the central nervous system, and sleepiness, mental sluggishness, and physical incoordination intensify.

Only rarely, however, will a normal, nonalcoholic drinker take in enough alcohol to lose consciousness. This is fortunate, for alcohol taken in large enough quantities to cause unconsciousness is dangerously near the amount needed to paralyze the respiratory center, shut off the breathing apparatus, and kill the drinker. As an anesthetic or pain killer, therefore, alcohol is inferior because it numbs the senses only at extremely high, nearly lethal doses. Stories from the old West about soldiers or cowboys facing amputation, gulping a lot of whiskey, and then screaming horribly when the doctor starts sawing demonstrate the point. The unfortunate patient may have succeeded in becoming drunk, but the alcohol did not obliterate his pain. Even a drunken Clint Eastwood winces when, in the movies, arrows and bullets are being removed from his body.

A Selectively Addicting Drug

Addiction-producing drugs, according to the World Health Organization (WHO), are those drugs which produce in the great majority of users an irresistible need for the drug, an increased tolerance to the effects of the drug, and physical dependence on the drug, manifested in severe and painful symptoms when the drug is withdrawn.[2] Examples are heroin, morphine, and codeine.

Heroin is addictive for almost 100 percent of its users; morphine is addictive for some 70 percent. With these drugs, addiction occurs after approximately four weeks of use, and the addict typically graduates to quantities well above the normally lethal dose, usually from twenty to one hundred times the initially effective dose.

Alcohol does not qualify as an addictive drug under the WHO guidelines simply because it causes addiction in only a minority—approximately 10 percent—of its users. Furthermore, addiction to alcohol for some requires a period of years, not weeks, to become established, and tolerance may be only three to four times greater in some alcoholics than in nonalcoholics.

It is also difficult to place alcohol in the category "habit-forming drug," defined by the WHO as a drug capable of causing an emotional or psychological (rather than physical) dependence in the user and which can be withdrawn without causing physical harm or pain. Of course, it does qualify in the limited sense that millions of people—alcoholics and nonalcoholics alike—become psychologically and emotionally dependent on it. However, alcohol does not fit snugly in this category because it does cause physical dependence in a minority of its users and those users definitely suffer both physical and mental anguish when the drug is withdrawn.

Alcohol, then, belongs in a category somewhere between the habit-forming and addiction-producing drugs. The WHO labelled it "intermediate in kind and degree" between the two categories of drugs, but even this label is inaccurate. *The fact is that the effects of alcohol simply cannot be generalized for both alcoholics and nonalcoholics.* For most drinkers, alcohol is not addictive; yet for the minority who are alcoholics, the criteria of true drug addiction are fulfilled: an increased tissue tolerance to the drug, a physical dependence on the drug with physical withdrawal symptoms, and an irresistible need for the drug when it is withdrawn.

The only way to clear up the confusion is to label alcohol a *selectively addicting drug*. It is addictive only for those individuals who are physically susceptible.

Alcohol the Food

Because alcohol contains calories, it is considered a food; and in terms of calories, it is a very rich food indeed. One ounce of pure alcohol delivers about 170 calories when broken down in the body. As Berton Roueché notes in *The Neutral Spirit*,

> That approximates the caloric vigor of a dozen Blue Point oysters, one broiled lamp chop, a hard roll, an average baked potato, a glass of milk, or a large orange. As a concentrated source of energy, alcohol thus ranks among the very richest of foods. Only the fats which assay around two hundred and seventy calories per ounce, are richer.[3]

Alcohol's calories are quickly available to the body and require the cells to do relatively little work to release them. Unlike most fats, proteins, and carbohydrates, which require one to four hours of soaking in the digestive acids secreted by the mouth, stomach, and small intestine, alcohol requires virtually no preparation before being absorbed into the bloodstream and distributed throughout the body. The breakdown process in the liver is relatively simple, and within minutes after ingestion alcohol's calories are supplying the body with a boost of energy. Unfortunately, these calories are empty, containing only tiny amounts of vitamins, minerals, and amino acids. Without sufficient amounts of these essential nutrients, the cells cannot replace damaged cell parts, create new cell materials, or carry on the normal everyday functions of a living, healthy cell.

Alcohol's energy "kick" is therefore its most beneficial and potentially its most deadly characteristic. As normally consumed, alcohol is usually in the body in small amounts and for relatively short periods of time, and its effects are therefore temporary. Furthermore, in small amounts, alcohol's benefits are noticeable and the penalties nonexistent: the cells receive a quick jolt of energy, the heartbeat accelerates, the brain cells speed up their communications, and the drinker feels euphoric and stimulated. The chemical causing these pleasurable effects is easily eliminated in an orderly and efficient manner, and the body then returns to normal activities. The brain cells quickly recover from their alcohol bath, the liver cells return to their everyday functions, nutritional materials once again flow in adequate proportions and amounts to the cells, and waste materials are efficiently eliminated.

In large and continuous amounts, however, the penalties of drinking far outweigh the initial benefits. The drinker is taking in so many calories from alcohol that he will automatically require fewer calories from other, more nutritious foods. Alcohol also disrupts the cells' ability to take in and use nutrients from other food. It interferes with the absorption of various vitamins from the gastrointestinal tract, inhibits the absorption of numerous amino acids, and increases the loss of certain vitamins in the urine, including thyamine, pyridoxine, and pantothenic acid. As a result, even if an alcoholic is eating well, alcohol denies him the full nutritional benefit of what he eats. Put another way, alcohol literally robs the body of those substances which are essential for life. Thus all alcoholics develop malnutrition regardless of what or how much they eat.

Anyone who has experienced the pleasant stimulating and euphoric effects of alcohol will find it easy to understand why over one hundred million people in the United States drink beverage alcohol. And there is certainly nothing complicated or mysterious about why alcoholics take up drinking, or why they continue to drink. The short answer is that they drink for all the reasons other people do—stimulation, euphoria, relaxation, and perhaps, mild intoxication. The significant question, then, is not why alcoholics drink, which is obvious, but why their motivation to drink becomes progressively stronger as they drink more, and more often. Once again, a look at the relevant facts will dispel any mysteries and provide a clear answer to this question.

3

What Makes
An Alcoholic:
Predisposing Factors

*In my judgment such of us who have never fallen
victims (to alcoholism) have been spared more by the
absence of appetite than from any mental or moral
superiority over those who have. Indeed, I believe if
we take habitual drunkards as a class, their heads
and their hearts will bear an advantageous compari-
son with those of any other class.*

Abraham Lincoln, Address to the
Washington Temperance Society, 1842

Over 100 million people in the United States drink
alcohol. Approximately 10 million of those drinkers are
alcoholic. What makes an alcoholic different from a
nonalcoholic? Does the alcoholic drink too much because his body is somehow abnormal, or does his body
become abnormal because he drinks too much? To
answer these questions, both the alcoholic's and the
nonalcoholic's reasons for drinking alcohol must be
examined.

Why People Drink Alcohol

The alcoholic starts drinking the same ways and for the same reasons the nonalcoholic starts drinking. He drinks to gain the effects of alcohol—to feel euphoric, stimulated, relaxed, or intoxicated. Sometimes he drinks to ease his frustrations; other times he drinks to put himself in a good mood. If he is tense, he may drink more than usual in an effort to unwind and get his mind off his troubles; if shy, he may drink to gain confidence; if extroverted, he may drink because he likes the company of other drinkers.

The alcoholic, like the nonalcoholic, is influenced in the way he drinks, where he drinks, how much, and how often he drinks by numerous psychological, social, or cultural factors. He may start drinking to impress his girl friend, to prove he is not afraid of his parent's disapproval, or because he is taunted into it by his friends. He may drink regularly because alcohol makes him laugh and forget his troubles or because he feels self-assured after a few drinks. If his wife has a cocktail every night, he may drink to keep her company. If his coworkers are heavy drinkers, he may learn to drink heavily.

Again like the nonalcoholic, the alcoholic learns to drink a variety of alcoholic beverages, and he develops preferences among beers, wines, and liquors. He learns how much and how fast people ordinarily drink on various occasions, and he learns how well he can "hold his liquor," how much it takes for him to feel good, to get high, or to get drunk.

Alcoholics as well as nonalcoholics may change their drinking habits because of life changes: death of a loved one, divorce, loss of a job. Loneliness, depression, fears and insecurities may also affect the way a person drinks. *The point is that none of these psychological or social factors are unique to either the alcoholic or nonalcoholic. Members of both groups drink together for the same reasons and with the same reinforcement by alcohol's stimulating and energizing effects.* The same variety of personality traits is found in both groups. Earlier advocates of an "alcoholic personality" have abandoned this hypothesis, and the theory of an "addictive personality" has also been discredited by lack of supportive evidence.

At some point, however, the drinking patterns of both groups begin to diverge. The alcoholic starts to drink more, and more often. He does not want to stop drinking once he has started. In the later stages of his drinking, he may keep a six pack of beer in his desk drawer or a pint of whiskey in the glove compartment. He may stop regularly at the corner tavern for a few quick ones after work. He may gulp his first drink or switch to martinis or straight whiskey.

Particular personality traits may become intensified or may undergo bizarre transformations. The sensitive may become insensitive, the extrovert introverted, the gentle violent, the tactful belligerent, and the compassionate uncaring. An early alcoholic is often irritable, moody, and depressed when he is not drinking. He angrily denies that he is drinking too much, blames his drinking on his nagging wife or his slave-driving boss, and stubbornly refuses to stop drinking. His promises to cut down are broken within days or weeks. His marriage slowly and painfully deteriorates, friendships dissolve, and interest in his work wanes.

The alcoholic appears to be using alcohol to solve his problems. His drinking appears to be an effort to drown his depression, forget work or marriage difficulties, obliterate loneliness and insecurities, and ease mounting tensions. *The reality, however, is very different from the appearance. In reality, an abnormal physiologi-*

cal reaction is causing the alcoholic's increasing psychological and emotional problems. Something has gone wrong inside.

Why Some People Are Alcoholic

Researchers have worked relentlessly, detectives on a tough case, to discover exactly what goes wrong. Their accumulated evidence shows that no one mysterious X factor causes alcoholism; no silver bullet exists which can be carefully extracted to make the alcoholic well again. Instead, their studies have uncovered a number of physiological differences between alcoholics and nonalcoholics. When taken together, these "predisposing factors" explain the alcoholic's vulnerability to alcohol and the onset of alcoholism.

The susceptible person must drink, of course, if he is to become addicted to alcohol. If he stops drinking for any reason—religious, cultural, social, or psychological—the disease is arrested. Furthermore, although psychological factors do not cause alcoholism, they can influence the alcoholic's attempts to control his drinking and his reaction to the addiction. A professional athlete trained to believe in the importance of health and fitness may go on the wagon repeatedly in an effort to halt his growing addiction to alcohol. When he starts drinking again, he may suffer crippling feelings of guilt and shame. A lonely and bored widow, on the other hand, may slide helplessly and resignedly into the disease, having few psychological or social incentives to help her fight the addiction.

In other words, while psychological, cultural, and social factors definitely influence the alcoholic's drinking patterns and behavior, they have no effect on whether or not he becomes alcoholic in the first place. *Physiology, not psychology, determines whether one drinker will become addicted to alcohol and another will not*. The alcoholic's enzymes, hormones, genes, and brain chemistry work together to create his abnormal and unfortunate reaction to alcohol. Discussions of the basic predisposing factors to alcoholism—abnormal metabolism, preference, heredity, prenatal influences, and ethnic susceptibilities—follow.

Abnormal Metabolism

Acetaldehyde, the intermediate byproduct of alcohol metabolism, appears to be one of the major villains in the onset of alcoholic drinking. The trouble probably begins in the liver. Charles Lieber, chief of the research program on liver disease and nutrition at the Bronx Veterans Administration Hospital, found that the same amount of alcohol produced very different blood acetaldehyde levels in alcoholics and nonalcoholics. Much higher levels were reached in alcoholics. Lieber theorized that this unusual buildup of acetaldehyde was caused in part by a malfunctioning of the liver's enzymes.[1]

Marc Schuckit, a psychiatrist and researcher at the University of California in San Diego, took this acetaldehyde difference in alcoholics one step further. His studies confirmed that, in alcoholics, the breakdown of acetaldehyde into acetate—the second step in alcohol metabolism—is performed at about half the rate of "normal," i.e., nonalcoholic, metabolism. It is this slowdown in metabolism which apparently causes acetaldehyde to accumulate.[2]

Both Lieber and Schuckit wanted to find out whether this enzyme malfunctioning was caused by heavy drinking or preceded heavy drinking. In other words, they hoped to answer the question: Does the alcoholic drink too much because his body is somehow abnormal or does his body become abnormal because he drinks too much? Lieber discovered that the liver mitochondria in alcoholics are abnormal and unable to change acetaldehyde into acetate at as great a rate as in nonalcoholics. Significantly, this low capacity was evident even in the early stages of heavy alcohol consumption, indicating that the alcoholic's cells are altered before he starts drinking heavily and continually.[3] Schuckit's studies with the offspring of alcoholics also indicate that the metabolic abnormality exists prior to heavy drinking. Like their alcoholic parents, the children of alcoholics (who before this experiment had never drunk alcohol) were unable to convert acetaldehyde to acetate at normal speed.[4] Heredity is clearly implicated in these studies.

Alcoholics, then, appear to have a liver cell malfunction which causes acetaldehyde to accumulate when they drink. Unfortunately for the alcoholic, acetaldehyde is a dangerous substance to have around in any quantity. Directly irritating to the cells and capable of hampering cellular activities, acetaldehyde can also react explosively when combined with other chemical substances. In the liver, Lieber suggests that the rising levels of acetaldehyde disturb many of the intricate activities of the cells, making it even more difficult for them to get rid of acetaldehyde, which, in turn, results in further damage to the cells. The cells may be permanently damaged if acetaldehyde is present in large quantities for long periods of time.

Moreover, acetaldehyde's harmful effects are not confined to the liver. High acetaldehyde levels can inhibit the synthesis of proteins in heart muscle, leading to impaired cardiac function. In the brain, a piling up of acetaldehyde can lead to bizarre and complicated chemical reactions. When acetaldehyde flows through the brain, it competes with other chemical substances known as brain amines (or neurotransmitters) for the attention of certain enzymes. Acetaldehyde wins this competition and, as a result, blocks the enzymes from accomplishing their primary duty of inhibiting the amines' activity.[5]

If acetaldehyde stopped interfering with the brain's chemical activities at this point, addiction to alcohol might never occur. Acetaldehyde, however, is a volatile substance which reacts with just about any other chemical which happens to be in the vicinity. The brain amines, which have been piling up while the acetaldehyde preoccupies their enzyme, interact with acetaldehyde to form compounds called "isoquinolines." These chemical agents are responsible for a number of fascinating and far-reaching events.

Like acetaldehyde, the isoquinolines suppress the enzyme which is responsible for deactivating many of the brain amines. The isoquinolines also release stored brain amines. In mice, they can aggravate alcohol withdrawal symptoms. For alcoholics, the isoquinolines have one characteristic which makes their other properties pale in significance. They are astonishingly like the opiates, and researchers suggest that they may act on the opiate receptors in the brain, thus contributing to the addiction of alcohol.[6]

In summary, addiction to alcohol may, in part, be traced back to a liver enzyme malfunction which results in a buildup of acetaldehyde throughout the body. In the brain, these large amounts of acetaldehyde interact with the brain amines to create the isoquinolines. These mischievous substances may trigger the alcoholic's need to drink more and more alcohol to counter the painful effects of the progressive buildup of acetaldehyde.

Preference for Alcohol

Everyone has a different reaction to the taste and effect of alcohol. Some people appear driven by the desire to drink; some enjoy the taste and effect and so drink whenever they have the chance; others like a drink every once in a while but prefer nonalcoholic beverages most of the time; still others feel sick to their stomachs, dizzy, flushed, or drunk after just one or two drinks. The last group will generally avoid drinking alcohol.

The same range of likes and dislikes for alcohol is found in rats and mice bred to be genetically alike. The DBA strain of mice, for example, are teetotallers. These animals probably find alcohol's taste or effect unpleasant. The C57BL strains, on the other hand, are heavy drinkers and will consistently choose an alcohol solution over a water or sugar and water solution. Other animals are more mixed in their likes and dislikes and can be compared to the typical social drinker who will slowly sip one or two drinks over the course of an evening.

Preference for alcohol is undoubtedly regulated by complicated chemical activities in the brain. In a 1968 experiment, rats dramatically reduced or completely stopped drinking alcohol when given a chemical substance which depleted the brain's supply of serotonin.[7] Serotonin, a brain amine responsible for relaying messages from one brain cell to another, appears to increase the animal's preference for alcohol. The brains of alcohol-seeking mice and rats, for example, contain higher levels of serotonin than the brains of alcohol-avoiding animals. Further, drinking alcohol increases serotonin concentrations in the brains of the animals that show a preference for alcohol but not in those which avoid it.[8]

Serotonin is only one of many chemical substances which regulate how much an animal will drink. Tetra-hydropapaveroline (THP), the product of the interaction of acetaldehyde and dopamine, a brain amine similar to serotonin, is another. When THP was injected into rats' brains, it caused rats that normally rejected alcohol to drink excessive amounts.[9] In what the experimenters called an "addictive-like intake," rats injected with THP drank to the point of intoxication and suffered withdrawal symptoms when they stopped drinking. They continued to drink as though to avoid the disagreeable and painful withdrawal symptoms. The animals' behavior, in short, mimicked the alcoholic's drinking behavior.

An animal's initial liking or dislike for alcohol is clearly only one factor involved in a biological predisposition to alcoholism. The THP study shows that preference is not even a necessary factor, since rats which at first refused to drink could be made to drink addictively when THP was injected into their brains. A number of chemical activities in the brain, therefore, appear to be at the roots of addictive drinking. Future research should further clarify the mechanisms of acetaldehyde, the brain amines, and the products of their interaction.

Heredity

Accumulated evidence clearly indicates that alcoholism is hereditary. Professionals and researchers, however, are often reluctant to accept heredity as a major cause of alcoholism, in part because they are committed to the common misconception that alcoholism is caused by social, cultural, and psychological factors. Genes may influence the alcoholic's reaction to alcohol, these professionals admit, but can genes explain every nuance of the alcoholic's behavior? What about his personal problems, including his troubled marriage, financial difficulties, emotional insecurities, and his belligerent refusal to stop drinking? People do not inherit functional, or nonorganic, psychological problems; therefore, if these problems are the causes of alcoholism, as many insist, then obviously alcoholism cannot be hereditary.

Once again, the consequences of alcoholism are confused with the causes. The weight of evidence clearly links alcoholism to heredity. In a recent study, psychiatrist and researcher Donald Goodwin provides clear and strong corroboration that alcoholism is, indeed, passed from parent to child through genes.[10] Goodwin was able to separate hereditary influences from environmental influences by studying the children of alcoholics who were taken from their parents at birth and adopted by nonrelatives. He postulated that if alcoholism were, indeed, inherited, these children would have a high rate of alcoholism even though they were not living with their biological alcoholic parent. If environmental influences were more important, the adopted child would be no more likely to become alcoholic than the children of nonalcoholic parents.

Goodwin found that the children of alcoholics do have a much higher risk of becoming alcoholics themselves—four times that of nonalcoholics—despite having no exposure to their alcoholic parent after the first weeks of life. They were also likely to develop the disease earlier in life, usually in their twenties. The children of nonalcoholic parents, on the other hand, showed relatively low rates of alcoholism even if reared by alcoholic foster parents.

In an effort to discover the relationship, if any, between alcoholic drinking and psychiatric problems, Goodwin compared the children of alcoholics with the children of nonalcoholics. The two groups were "virtually indistinguishable" with regard to depression, anxiety neurosis, personality disturbance, psychopathology, criminality, and drug abuse. As already indicated, psychiatric problems are clearly not relevant to the onset of alcoholism.

In a second adoption study, Goodwin compared the sons of alcoholics who were adopted and raised by an unrelated family with their brothers who had been raised by the alcoholic parent. He found that the children raised by the biological alcoholic parent were no more likely to become alcoholic than their brothers who were raised by nonrelatives.

These astonishing findings shatter those theories which insist that the children of alcoholics become alcoholics themselves because they learn bad habits from their parents or model their behavior on that of their alcoholic parent. They also destroy one other misconception—the belief that problem drinking and alcoholism are directly related. The terms "alcohol abuse and alcoholism" are commonly used to imply that the former causes the latter. Most people believe problem drinkers, or those people who use alcohol to solve personal problems, become alcoholics. Problem drinkers, the theory goes, abuse alcohol because they are unhappy, lonely, depressed, angry, hostile, unemployed, divorced, poor, or generally dissatisfied with life. As they drink more and more often for relief, they become addicted to alcohol.

Goodwin not only failed to find this connection between alcoholism and problem drinking; he found an inverse relationship: the children of nonalcoholic parents had a much lower rate of alcoholism but were more likely to be heavy or problem drinkers. As Goodwin summarized the results, "Our findings tend to contradict the oft-repeated assertion that alcoholism results from the interaction of multiple causes—social, psychological, biological. . . . The 'father's sins' may be visited on the sons even in the father's absence."[11] Problem drinking, then, appears to be caused by psychological, emotional, or social problems, while alcoholic drinking is caused by hereditary factors.*

Goodwin's studies provide compelling evidence that alcoholics do not drink addictively because they are depressed, lonely, immature, or dissatisfied. They drink addictively because they have inherited a physical susceptibility to alcohol which results in addiction if they drink. Furthermore, this evidence has profound implications for treatment. While it may be possible to teach

---

*Making a clear differentiation between alcoholism and problem drinking is a major theme of this book and is discussed in more detail in chapter 11.

the problem drinker how to drink in a more responsible way, the alcoholic's drinking is controlled by physiological factors which cannot be altered through psychological methods such as counseling, threats, punishment, or reward. In other words, the alcoholic is powerless to control his reaction to alcohol.

Prenatal Influences

When a pregnant woman drinks, the fetus drinks with her. If the mother drinks too much, so does the fetus. The fetus, of course, has no defenses against these large doses of alcohol. The fetal alcohol syndrome (FAS), in which the children of alcoholic mothers suffer from mental retardation, stunted growth, and facial disfigurations such as flattened noses and narrowed eyes, is a well-known and documented reaction of the vulnerable fetus to large and continuous doses of alcohol.

Since alcoholism is hereditary, the fetus that is subjected to large amounts of alcohol may also become addicted while still in the womb. When the baby is born and the umbilical cord supplying alcohol is severed, the newborn child may experience withdrawal symptoms. As one researcher describes it:

> The alcoholic mother who has been drinking heavily through pregnancy and particularly that mother who has actually had acute alcoholic withdrawal during pregnancy may have ingested sufficient alcohol to have developed incipient signs and symptoms of tolerance and physical dependence in the newborn child. . . . Such a child, in addition to having the hypothesized genetic propensity toward alcoholism has probably been exposed to high levels of alcohol during his intrauterine development. Such a child may actually have developed some level

of tolerance and physical dependence during pregnancy and may be born—in a manner similar to that of children of heroine addicts—in an acute alcoholic withdrawal state.[12]

The newborn is, in fact, an alcoholic. Years later when he takes his "first" drink, he may experience an instant reactivation of this addiction. Many alcoholics do appear to be instantly addicted to alcohol from their very first drink, experiencing immediate tolerance changes, craving for alcohol, and withdrawal symptoms when they stop drinking. This "instant alcoholic" may actually have triggered an addiction that began before he was born.

Ethnic Susceptibilities to Alcohol

Extreme differences in alcoholism rates have been found among various ethnic groups. For example, Jews and Italians have low alcoholism rates, about 1 percent, while at the other extreme, Native Americans have extraordinarily high rates, somewhere around 80–90 percent. Once again, physical factors—not psychological, social, or cultural factors—explain these different ethnic susceptibilities to alcohol.

Dr. Bert Vallee and his colleagues at Harvard Medical School have been studying biochemical and genetic aspects of alcoholism. They have isolated fifteen different forms of the alcohol dehydrogenase (ADH) liver enzyme and discovered that the number and variety of these enzymes vary widely from person to person. The complex patterns appear to be genetically controlled, and different racial groups have a typical variation of the number and type of these "isoenzymes." Vallee suspects that each combination of isoenzymes reacts with alcohol differently and determines the person's specific physiological response. Flushing, nausea, violent behavior, sleepiness, and hyperactivity, for example, are probably brought about by the drinker's specific grouping of isoenzymes.[13]

Vallee's findings help to explain the abundance of research showing different physiological reactions to alcohol among various ethnic groups. Fenna, for example, discovered that a group of Native Americans were unable to oxidize and eliminate alcohol as quickly as Caucasians; and Wolff found that Japanese, Koreans, and Taiwanese had aversive reactions including flushing and mild to moderate intoxication with alcohol doses causing no obvious reaction in the majority of Caucasians. He ruled out the possibility that this reaction was acquired or learned by testing Oriental and Caucasian newborn infants and finding similar responses.[14] Researchers have also found higher levels of acetaldehyde, alcohol's highly toxic breakdown product, in Orientals than in Caucasians after drinking alcohol.[15] These high acetaldehyde levels are probably the result of enzyme deficiencies; the flushing and nausea that result could explain why Orientals tend to drink sparingly or not at all.

Another interesting finding of recent research is the discovery that a direct relationship exists between the length of time an ethnic group has been exposed to alcohol and the rate of alcoholism within that group. Jews and Italians, for example, have had access to large amounts of alcohol for more than 7,000 years, and their alcoholism rate is very low. Alcohol was first introduced in quantity to the northern European countries, including France, Ireland, and the Scandinavian countries, some 1,500 years ago, and the rates of alcoholism are relatively higher there. Native Americans, who suffer from extremely high alcoholism rates, did not have large supplies of alcohol until approximately 300 years ago.[16]

These differences in susceptibility are exactly what we should expect given the fact that alcoholism is a hereditary disease. The implication is that the longer an

Ethnic Group	Time Exposure	Susceptibility to Alcoholism	Alcoholism Rate
Jews, Italians	7,000 + years	Low	Low
Scandinavians, Irish, French	1,500 years	Medium	Medium
North American Indians, Eskimos	300 years	High	High

From James R. Milam, *The Emergent Comprehensive Concept of Alcoholism*, 1974. (Out of print)

ethnic group is exposed to alcohol, the lower its members' susceptibility to alcoholism. This relationship is consistent with the principle of natural selection whereby those people with a high genetic susceptibility are eliminated over many generations, resulting in a lower susceptibility rate for the entire group. People with low susceptibility to alcoholism survive and pass on their low susceptibility. Thus, the rate of alcoholism among high susceptibility groups such as Native Americans should lower significantly over time if they continue to drink.

Interbreeding among ethnic groups will also have a dramatic effect on alcoholism rates. If ethnic groups with high susceptibility rates interbreed with ethnic groups with a lower susceptibility, the alcoholism rates for both groups will change. In fact, it has been observed that alcoholism rates among both Jews and Italians are rising steadily as they increasingly interbreed with peoples who have a higher susceptibility to alcoholism.

The scientific evidence clearly indicates an interplay of various hereditary, physiological factors—metabolic, hormonal, and neurological—which work together and in tandem to determine the individual's susceptibility to alcoholism. It would be a mistake to simplify the interactions in the body, making it appear that one specific gene, one enzyme, or one hormone is solely responsible for a chain of events leading in a straight line to physical dependence and addiction. Even a slight difference in the number or type of liver enzymes, for example, could alter a person's drinking patterns, preference, and problems. Yet, while additional predisposing factors to alcoholism will undoubtedly be discovered, abundant knowledge already exists to confirm that alcoholism is a hereditary, physiological disease and to account fully for its onset and progression.

4

The Early, Adaptive Stage of Alcoholism

It (alcoholic beverages) sloweth age, it strengtheneth youth, it helpeth digestion, it abandoneth melancholie, it relisheth the heart, it lighteneth the mind, it quickeneth the spirits, it keepeth and preserveth the head from whirling, the eyes from dazzling, the tongue from lisping, the mouth from snaffling, the teeth from chattering, and the throat from rattling; it keepeth the stomach from wambling, the heart from swelling, the hands from shivering, the sinews from shrinking, the veins from crumbling, the bones from aching, and the marrow from soaking.

Anonymous, thirteenth century

One of the first symptoms of alcoholism is, ironically and tragically, an ability to increase alcohol intake and still function "normally." It is ironic because most diseases incur immediate and obvious penalties, not benefits, and result in reduced functioning rather than improvement in functioning. But in the early stages of alcoholism, the alcoholic is not sick, in pain, or visibly abnormal. In fact, the early, adaptive stage of alcoholism appears to be marked by the opposite of disease, for the alcoholic is "blessed" with a supernormal ability to tolerate alcohol and enjoy its euphoric and stimulating effects.

This improvement of functioning is tragic because the alcoholic has little or no warning of the deterioration inevitably to follow. Neither the early stage alcoholic nor his friends have reason to suspect that he is suffering from a progressive and often fatal disease. The disease is difficult to recognize or diagnose in its early stages because the symptoms are so subtle and so easily confused with normal reactions to alcohol. No pain or visible malfunction is involved. The early alcoholic does not complain, has no reason to visit a doctor because of his drinking, and does not suffer when he drinks. Indeed, he appears to be just like all other drinkers. He has hangovers when he overdrinks, but so do his friends. He enjoys drinking, but so do his friends. He looks forward to his evening cocktails, but so do his friends.

In this early stage, it would be difficult if not impossible to convince the alcoholic to stop drinking. Why should he stop if he does not feel sick but in fact feels better when he drinks? An early stage alcoholic confronted with a diagnosis of alcoholism and the advice to stop drinking would probably respond, "Who are you kidding? Me, an alcoholic? I can drink more than my friends, I rarely get a hangover, I'm never belligerent or violent, I never miss work, I don't drink in the morning, I can stop whenever I want, and I feel terrific when I drink. Go pick on someone who really has a problem!"

Because the early alcoholic shows no sign of disease, the logical but wholly mistaken idea persists that alcoholism begins only when the drinker does suffer from drinking and does show some deterioration in physiological functioning, such as severe withdrawal symptoms, personality disintegration, or inability to control his intake. Before these visible symptoms appear, most people assume that alcoholics and nonalcoholics experience precisely the same physical reaction to alcohol.

In fact, they do not. The alcoholic reacts physically in an abnormal way to alcohol, and his disease begins long before he behaves or thinks like an alcoholic. The reactions or adaptations of the body's cells to alcohol remain hidden in the early stages of the disease, but they are nevertheless happening. In months or years, the cells will have been so altered by alcohol that the alcoholic's behavior and thought processes will be affected. Then the disease will no longer be hidden, and the alcoholic will clearly be in trouble with alcohol.

In the early stage, however, the disease is subtle and difficult to recognize. It is characterized by adaptations in the liver and central nervous system, increased tolerance to alcohol, and improved performance when drinking.

Adaptation

A general biological rule holds that when any bodily system is under stress it either adapts or suffers damage. Adaptation is actually a tool of survival, helping the body endure stressful changes in internal or external environments. Adaptational responses occur rapidly, spontaneously, and in most cases, without the person's conscious knowledge. To cite the obvious example, muscles that are stressed grow and get stronger—a fundamental principle of exercise. Overstress, of course, will damage the muscles.

In the onset of alcoholism, adaptation is central. Alcoholics initially experience physical stress whenever they drink. Their enzymes, hormones, and numerous chemical processes are thrown out of balance by alcohol, and the normal ebb and flow of materials into and out of the cells is upset. To counteract this confusion, the cells make certain changes in their structures. These adaptations gradually allow the cells to work smoothly and efficiently even when alcohol is present in the body in large quantities. In fact, the alcoholic's cells become so competent at using alcohol for energy that they choose alcohol over other energy, or food, sources.

For the alcoholic, however, alcohol is a distinctly unlovable and ungrateful guest. Although it gives the cells a rich supply of energy and provides stimulation and sedation in different amounts, these benefits are inevitably turned into stiff penalties. Gradually alcohol attacks the cells, destroying their delicate chemical balances, eating away at the membranes, and deforming the cell innards. If the alcoholic continues to drink, the penalties of drinking sooner or later outweigh the benefits as the alcoholic gradually progresses into the later, deteriorative stages of the disease. The length of time between adaptation and deterioration varies from one alcoholic to the next. For some alcoholics, adaptation occurs rapidly, and within weeks or months after first taking a drink, the alcoholic is clearly addicted to alcohol. In other cases, many years go by before the earliest symptoms of adaptation and addiction develop.

The critical point, however, is this: the preliminary adaptation begins before the alcoholic starts drinking heavily and, in fact, causes the heavier drinking. Adaptation does not occur because a person drinks too much. On the contrary, when a person starts drinking more, and more often, and the pattern persists, he is displaying one of the first symptoms of alcoholism.

The adaptations which occur in the early stage of alcoholism are of two kinds: those affecting the metabolism of alcohol, and those taking place in the central nervous system and contributing to addiction. Both types of adaptation have direct effects on the alcoholic's ability to drink large amounts of alcohol without becoming intoxicated (tolerance) and actually to function better when he is drinking than when he is not drinking (improved performance).

Metabolic Adaptations

Metabolic adaptations take place primarily in the liver where most alcohol metabolism takes place. But the brain is also capable of metabolizing small amounts of alcohol, and evidence suggests that the brain's metabolic activity, like the liver's, increases through various adaptive changes.

The Microsomal Ethanol Oxidizing System (MEOS). In most alcoholic and nonalcoholic drinkers, the alcohol dehydrogenase (ADH) pathway (operating primarily in the liver) eliminates approximately two-thirds of the alcohol present in the body. Because of a liver enzyme abnormality, however, alcoholics are unable to eliminate the alcohol breakdown product acetaldehyde as quickly as nonalcoholics (see the discussion in the previous chapter). As a result, acetaldehyde builds up and threatens the cells with its toxic effects.

The liver has an amazing capacity to adjust and adapt, and when necessary, it apparently gears up an additional system for processing alcohol. This system has been identified by Charles Lieber as "the microsomal ethanol oxidizing system," or MEOS.[1] In alcoholics, MEOS adapts by increasing its activity—the enzymes responsible for oxidizing alcohol are increased, and new cells are created. As a result, the alcoholic's ability to convert alcohol into acetaldehyde also increases.

Unfortunately, the ability to get rid of the resulting acetaldehyde does not keep pace. MEOS actually compounds the alcoholic's problems rather than solving them, because it increases his ability to tolerate and process very large doses of alcohol and yet does not sufficiently improve his ability to eliminate acetaldehyde.*

---

*People who have a high level of acetaldehyde without the ability to tolerate and process very large doses of alcohol may develop an aversion to alcohol and drink sparingly or not at all. This may explain why Orientals with high acetaldehyde levels avoid alcohol rather than adapt to it.

Most of the incoming alcohol is still directed to the deficient ADH pathway. Thus, both MEOS and the ADH pathway produce ever-increasing levels of acetaldehyde. A vicious circle begins when the alcoholic must drink more to maintain a level of alcohol sufficient to override and block the devastating effects of the rising level of acetaldehyde. This is the basis of the alcoholic's "physiological imperative" to keep drinking once he starts that is regularly mistaken for a psychological compulsion to drink.

The Mitochondria. The mitochondria are tiny structures within each cell which are responsible for releasing energy from food. Since alcohol contains a richer supply of energy than most foods and since this energy is easily released, alcohol is a ready source of fuel.

In alcoholics, the mitochondria apparently attempt to capitalize on this rich energy source by changing their structure to accommodate large amounts of alcohol. Normal mitochondria are round with clearly defined outer walls and inner structures; in alcoholics, the mitochondria become enlarged and misshapen, and their inner architecture is redesigned. These adaptations may, in part, be an attempt by the mitochondria to enable the body to process more alcohol so it can benefit from alcohol's abundant and readily available energy.

Unfortunately, for all that alcohol gives the cells, it eventually takes much more away. Electron micrographs of chronic alcoholics' liver cells depict an eerie battleground: the mitochondria are scattered haphazardly, some grotesquely misshapen, others with gaping holes in their membranes, and still others white and vacant, bled dry of everything inside. Once again, it seems that the cells' early adaptations support the heavier drinking that eventually leads to widespread cell injury and death.

Central Nervous System Adaptations in the Cell Membranes

The cell membranes are more than simple walls keeping the vital parts of the cell from leaking out. They are actually complex chemical and electrical doorways which let various substances into the cells while denying access to others and which allow wastes to be eliminated from the cell. In a sense, they are the guardians of the cell, protecting the vulnerable cell materials which are vital to life. The membranes' activities ultimately affect everything that goes on inside and outside the cell.

Not surprisingly, the balance of incoming and outgoing elements is critically important to the health and vitality of the cell. Nutrients must get into the cell in adequate amounts and proportions to allow the cell to make repairs, feed itself, and stay healthy and strong. Waste materials must be eliminated quickly and properly, or the cell will become poisoned with its own wastes. Enzymes, hormones, fats, and proteins must all be let into the cells at the right time and in the correct amounts or the cells' orderly functioning will be threatened. Since cells are the building blocks of tissues, and tissues are the building blocks of the major organs, any injury to the cells will eventually be felt throughout the body.

Alcohol consumption interferes drastically with the normal events going on within and across the cell membranes. It changes the chemical structure of the cell membranes, forcing certain materials to be imprisoned within the cell while letting other vital materials escape. For nonalcoholics, alcohol causes only minor inconveniences for the cells. In low doses, alcohol actually stimulates the cell membranes and causes the release of various chemicals which contribute to euphoria, excitement, and pleasurable sensations. In large doses, alcohol temporarily depresses the cell membranes' activities, leading to the abnormal behavior associated with drunkenness.

When alcohol is taken in large amounts over long periods of time, however, the cell membranes adapt by developing methods of coping with these large doses of alcohol. In experiments with rats made tolerant to and physically dependent on alcohol, the cell membranes showed an increased resistance to alcohol's toxic effects. The membranes actually toughened up in an apparent effort to remain stable when alcohol was present in large quantities. Researchers conclude that large and continuous doses of alcohol stimulate the cells to adjust the structure and thus the functioning of their membranes.[2] The cells now welcome alcohol and adjust to its toxic aftereffects. As a result, the cells are able to cope with increasingly large doses of alcohol; they become, in other words, tolerant to alcohol.

If the alcoholic continues to drink in large quantities, however, the toughened membranes are continually battered and gradually damaged by alcohol's poisonous aftereffects. They weaken and, in some cases, dissolve. No longer able to function as selective doorways, the membranes now let poisonous substances into the cells while vital fluids and enzymes leak out. The results are catastrophic. Vital chemical processes are interrupted or altered, and throughout the body, cells sicken and die. The destruction of cell membranes is linked with many of the conditions which afflict alcoholics in the late stage of their disease, including severe withdrawal symptoms, such as convulsions, hallucinations, and delirium tremens, and damage to the heart muscle (alcoholic cardiomyopathy).

Deterioration is a slow and gradual process, however, and despite the destruction which inevitably comes later, adaptation in the early stage of alcoholism is initially responsible for an acceleration, not a slowdown, of functioning. The alcoholic's cells are better able to cope with alcohol and withstand its toxic effects. The first visible indication that adaptation has occurred is the phenomenon called tolerance.

Tolerance

The word tolerance has many meanings. To most people, tolerance denotes a capacity to consume large amounts of alcohol without passing out or feeling nauseated. "He has an amazing tolerance for the stuff," an admirer might comment about someone who consistently drinks everyone else under the table and then proceeds to drive home safely.

This interpretation is not quite accurate, for tolerance is actually a term which applies to all drinkers. Every drinker has a specific tolerance to alcohol. Below his tolerance level, the drinker can function more or less normally; at levels above his tolerance threshold, he will act intoxicated. Tolerance is therefore a condition that can only be measured accurately in a laboratory where the drinker's blood level and behavior can be carefully monitored.

Nonalcoholics fairly quickly establish a stable tolerance level which may be high or low. Alcoholics, however, typically experience a dramatic climb in tolerance in the first stage of alcoholism and can often drink huge amounts of alcohol without showing obvious impairment of their ability to walk, talk, think, and react. Anyone who observes the early- and middle-stage alcoholic's drinking behavior is familiar with the fact that the typical alcoholic can drink as much as a liter of wine, a dozen beers, or even a bottle of whiskey without acting drunk.

This ability to tolerate large amounts of alcohol can develop over a period of weeks or years, depending on the individual. Some alcoholics experience a subtle, gradual shift from normal drinking to a drinking pattern of increased frequency and stepped-up amounts over a period of many years. Most alcoholics, however, experience a more immediate change in their tolerance level and are able to drink more than their friends and show less impairment soon after they first start drinking.

Regardless of how long it takes to develop increased tolerance, the same adaptational processes underlie its development. Adaptations in the MEOS and the mitochondria are basically responsible for increased *metabolic tolerance*, which is evident in the alcoholic's ability to metabolize alcohol more quickly and efficiently. *Cellular or tissue tolerance* is the result of central nervous system adaptations to alcohol's toxic effects and is evident in the alcoholic's ability to drink large amounts of alcohol without becoming intoxicated. As one research team described it, tissue tolerance indicates "a change in the nervous system leading to *improvement of physiological functioning* in the presence of a given concentration of alcohol" (italics added).[3]

Two major misconceptions about the phenomenon of tolerance should be straightened out. The first is the belief that tolerance is a learned response. Many people think that the more the alcoholic drinks, the more he learns how to compensate for the effects of drinking. But tolerance is not learned, nor is it subject to the alcoholic's conscious control or will power. Tolerance is caused by physiological changes which occur primarily in the liver and central nervous system. These changes cause alterations in the alcoholic's brain's electrical impulses, its hormone and enzyme levels, and the chemical structure of cell membranes, all of which contribute to tolerance. Learned behavior cannot possibly account for these physiological and biochemical functions.

The second and very misleading misconception is that tolerance initially develops because the person drinks too much. Many alcoholism theorists and professionals insist that psychological or emotional problems are the cause of increased drinking; as the person drinks more frequently, they conclude, he runs the risk of becoming tolerant to alcohol. Again, the implication is that alcoholics are responsible for contracting their disease—by drinking too much, they make themselves tolerant to alcohol. Yet the opposite is true. Tolerance is actually responsible for the alcoholic's continued and increasingly large intake of alcohol. In fact, an increase in the amount and frequency of drinking is the typical symptom of a developing tolerance to alcohol and one of the first warning signs of alcoholism.

When the alcoholic becomes tolerant to alcohol's effects, he is responding to changes which are occurring inside him. He is not responsible for initiating these changes. He is not even conscious that these changes are taking place.

Improved Performance

In this early, hidden stage of alcoholism, the only visible difference between the alcoholic and the nonalcoholic is improved performance in the alcoholic when he drinks and a deterioration in performance when he stops drinking. His improved performance is the result of metabolic and tissue tolerance to alcohol's effects, as mentioned in the previous section. The chart below illustrates the dramatic differences in physiological functioning between alcoholics and nonalcoholics when they drink and then stop drinking.

When the typical nonalcoholic drinks, his physical and psychological functioning improve with approximately one-half ounce to one ounce of alcohol. He experiences feelings of euphoria, relaxation, and well-being. His performance is slightly better than normal. Concentration, memory, attention span, creative thinking, are all improved with an ounce or less of alcohol.

The stimulating and energizing effects of a small amount of alcohol are offset, however, by the sedative effects brought on by additional drinking, and the nonalcoholic's performance soon falls below the normal level. If the nonalcoholic continues to drink, his blood alcohol level (BAL) rises even higher, and his behavior rapidly deteriorates. He slurs his words, has difficulty walking, and his memory and thinking abilities gradually worsen. When the nonalcoholic stops drinking, his BAL slowly descends toward normal, and his behavior also gradually returns to normal.

Psychological and
Physiological Functioning

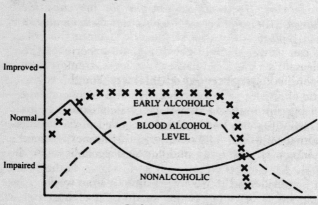

Performance over Time

Something completely different happens when the early-stage alcoholic drinks. Alcoholics in the early, adaptive stage of their disease also show improvement of functioning as the blood alcohol level begins to rise. But unlike the nonalcoholic, this improvement continues with additional drinking. Even when blood alcohol remains at fairly high levels—levels which would overwhelm the nonalcoholic, causing him to stumble, stutter,

58

and sway—the early alcoholic is often able to talk coherently, walk a straight line, or skillfully maneuver a car.[4] Only when the alcoholic stops drinking and his BAL descends, does his performance deteriorate—and it does so very rapidly.

Understanding the relationship between alcohol and improved performance is crucial to an understanding of alcoholic behavior. The alcoholic's increasing motivation to drink, for example, can be partially explained by alcohol's "normalizing" effect on his behavior and emotions.[5] Because alcohol immediately makes the alcoholic feel better, think clearly, and act normally, another drink is the specific preventive for a drop in blood alcohol level and a corresponding drop in performance.

The therapeutic effects of alcohol may last for prolonged periods of time, provided the alcoholic drinks within his tolerance limit. If he drinks more than his cells can handle, he will get drunk and experience the unpleasant symptoms of nausea, dizziness, tremors, loss of coordination, and confused thinking. For the therapeutic effect, he must keep his BAL at a fairly constant level by continuing to drink; if he stops drinking, his BAL will drop and both psychological and physiological performance will rapidly deteriorate. Mike's experience is common for early and middle-stage alcoholics:

> Friday night Mike went directly from work to his favorite tavern for an evening of beer and pool. He drank steadily from 6 p.m. to 1 a.m., but he never felt or acted drunk. In fact, he dominated the pool table, winning every game.
>
> When he left the tavern and started home, Mike felt fine. He was clear-headed, mentally alert, and physically in control. Friends who saw him leave later told him they had no idea he was drunk.
>
> After 15 or 20 minutes on the road,

however, he began to feel slightly weak and nauseated. He was driving erratically when the police stopped him. When he tried to walk a straight line, he was dizzy and confused. The tests were repeated at the police station an hour later, and Mike could barely stand on two feet let alone balance on one. He seemed to be getting drunker and drunker, and the arresting officer decided to lock him up for the night, blaming his deteriorating condition on the delayed effects of alcohol. "He drank too much, and it finally caught up with him," he decided.

Mike was later charged with drunk driving. Because it was his first offense, the judge dismissed the charges on the condition that he enter alcoholism treatment. At his first session, Mike was both embarrassed and bewildered. "I don't understand it," he told the counselor. "I felt just fine at the tavern. I was thinking straight and playing terrific pool. When I stopped drinking and headed for home, I was suddenly drunk and out of control. What happened?"

When Mike was drinking at the tavern, he was able to talk coherently, play a competitive game of pool, and continue to drink steadily without being drunk—even though his BAL was as high as .20, which would cause severe motor disturbances in most nonalcoholics. It was when Mike left the bar and stopped drinking that his BAL began to descend, and his physiological and psychological functioning rapidly deteriorated. In other words, not until he stopped drinking did he feel drunk, sick, shaky, and out of control. The same cells which were able to function well as long as the BAL was ascending or staying level, were unable to function normally as soon as the BAL started to drop. Not only could these cells handle large amounts of alcohol; they actually needed it to function normally. They were, in fact, addicted to alcohol.

Most alcoholics discover "maintenance drinking" early on in their drinking careers, and they learn ways to protect themselves against the disastrous drop in blood alcohol level. One recovered alcoholic, when told of Mike's experience, said, "If Mike continues to drink, he will learn fast enough. Either he'll keep a bottle in the car to maintain him until he gets home, or he'll pick a tavern closer to home and gulp a last drink just before leaving." Maintenance drinking is not gluttony or irresponsible drinking, but a protective device whereby the alcoholic delays the drop in BAL until he is safely off the road and back in bed. By drinking continuously but never overdrinking, he attempts to hold on to the benefits of drinking while forestalling the penalties.

Tragically, the alcoholic can only temporarily control his drinking behavior. Over a period of years, the cells' dependence on alcohol becomes more firmly entrenched until, at some point, the alcoholic no longer has a choice. He needs alcohol to function, and he suffers terribly when he stops drinking. The benefits of adaptation are gradually overshadowed by the penalties of deterioration.

5

The Middle Stage
of Alcoholism

"One thing about alcohol, it works. It may destroy a man's career, ruin his marriage, turn him into a zombie unconscious in a hallway—but it works. On short term, it works much faster than a psychiatrist or a priest or the love of a husband or a wife. Those things... they all take time. They must be developed. . . . But alcohol is always ready to go to work at once. Then minutes, half an hour, the little formless fears are gone or turned into harmless amusement. But they come back. Oh yes, and they bring reinforcements."

From *Carlotta McBride*,
a fictional study of an alcoholic
by Charles Orson Gorman

There is no actual cutoff line between early and middle stages of alcoholism, but there are several characteristic features that signal a new stage in the progression of the disease. As physiological changes gradually occur, the penalties of drinking begin to outweigh the benefits. Pleasurable drinking for a "high," a lift in feeling and performance from a relatively normal base, gives way to a more urgent "drinking for medicine" to "cure" the pain and misery caused by previous drinking. The basic cause of the increase in penalties is deterioration. Organs and systems that once welcomed the large doses of alcohol and tolerated its toxic aftereffects are being damaged. Now when the alcoholic stops drinking, his suffering is more severe and prolonged.

As the withdrawal symptoms intensify, the alcoholic relieves his physical and psychological pain with more alcohol, which inevitably makes the withdrawal symptoms worse. The alcoholic's every action, mood, and emotion is increasingly governed by his need to drink. This physiological need for alcohol is often referred to as "craving." A spiral of drinking, suffering, and drinking again gradually progresses to the point where the alcoholic is no longer able to control his drinking consistently. Noticeable loss of control helps define the end of the middle stage and the beginning of the later, deteriorative stage of alcoholism.

The middle stage of alcoholism, then, can be characterized by three basic features: *physical dependence* as experienced in acute and protracted withdrawal syndromes; *craving;* and *loss of control.* These features deserve careful examination.

Physical Dependence

In the adaptive stage, when the cells of the central nervous system change their functioning to accommodate alcohol, the alcoholic's tolerance increases, and he is able to drink greater quantities of alcohol without becoming drunk. As he drinks more, and more often, to get the desired effect, the cells of his body are soaked in alcohol for long periods of time. The cell membranes become increasingly resistant to alcohol's effects, and the mitochondria within the cells increase in size and shift functions in order to accommodate the alcohol. With these changes, the adapted cells are able to live and thrive in an environment where alcohol is continually present in large amounts.

This situation continues as long as the alcoholic does not drink more than his cells can process—in other words, as long as he drinks within his tolerance—and as long as he continues drinking. If the alcoholic overdrinks his tolerance, the cells will be overwhelmed, and he will get drunk. If he stops drinking, the addicted cells will suddenly be thrown into a state of acute distress. They have become unable to function normally without alcohol. The cells' distress when alcohol is no longer present in the body, or when the BAL is falling, is evident in various symptoms known as "the withdrawal syndrome." Withdrawal symptoms demonstrate that physical dependence exists; they are the visible signs of addiction.

The withdrawal syndrome occurs in two phases: the *acute withdrawal syndrome*, which is experienced immediately after the alcoholic stops drinking and lasts up to a few days; and the *protracted withdrawal syndrome*, which lasts for months and even years of abstinence if the alcoholic's nutritional balance is not restored. Most people are familiar with the acute withdrawal syndrome, but the protracted withdrawal syndrome is not so well known or appreciated. Yet a complete understanding of alcoholism is impossible without an understanding of the nature and progression of these related syndromes. The acute withdrawal syndrome helps to explain why the alcoholic is in such mental and physical distress immediately after he stops drinking and why the urge for a drink is overpowering; the protracted withdrawal syndrome explains why the alcoholic continues to be depressed, shaky, and irritable many days, months, or even years after his last drink, and why so many alcoholics return to drinking after a period of sobriety.

The Acute Withdrawal Syndrome

One of the most confusing aspects of alcoholism is that *the alcoholic is most sick, not when he drinks, but when he stops drinking*. His body has adapted to the constant presence of alcohol—his cells are accustomed to functioning with alcohol as their major source of energy and stimulation and as an antidote for the ever-present toxicity.

Thus, when the alcoholic stops drinking, all hell breaks loose. Blood vessels constrict, cutting down on the flow of blood and oxygen to the cells. The blood glucose level drops sharply and remains unstable. The brain amines serotonin and norepinephrine decrease dramatically. Hormones, enzymes, and body fluid levels fluctuate erratically. The body's cells are malnourished and toxic from long exposure to large doses of alcohol and acetaldehyde.

These chaotic events cause fundamental disruptions in the brain's chemical and electrical activity. As soon as the blood alcohol level begins to descend, the brain cells, or neurons, become excited and agitated. The entire brain is affected, as the sensitive neurons send out highly disorganized and chaotic distress signals. The brain is, in a sense, short-circuiting, and the resulting pandemonium creates numerous psychological and physiological problems for the alcoholic, including profound mental confusion, memory defects, lack of muscular coordination, convulsions, hallucinations, paranoia, violent or fearful behavior—all the symptoms associated with the acute withdrawal syndrome.

In early-stage alcoholics, the major withdrawal symptoms are anxiety, tremors, and agitation—symptoms which many nonalcoholics also experience after a night of heavy drinking. As the disease progresses, however, the alcoholic's withdrawal symptoms become more and more severe, and he may eventually suffer from the alcoholic hangover, convulsions, hallucinations, and delirium tremens (DT's). The withdrawal symptoms vary according to how much the alcoholic drinks, and how long he continues to drink without stopping. In general, the more the alcoholic drinks, the more he will suffer when he stops drinking; if he drinks for a week, he will suffer more than if he drinks for one or two days. Furthermore, the frequency, duration, and intensity of the symptoms vary from one alcoholic to the next, depending on constitutional differences, malnutrition, and other diseases or medical complications. The simultaneous or alternate use of other drugs can also increase the severity of the acute withdrawal syndrome.

Early Symptoms of Withdrawal. Often the first evidence of the alcoholic withdrawal syndrome is a shaky and agitated feeling the morning after drinking and the growing desire for a remedy for these symptoms. In the early alcoholic, the cells are mildly agitated when alcohol is withdrawn. While the symptoms are uncomfortable and unpleasant, they last for a relatively short time and are not incapacitating. The alcoholic in mild withdrawal can get out of bed, give a speech, and play a game of racquetball at the end of the day with no major difficulties.

Other mild withdrawal symptoms experienced by almost all early-stage alcoholics include nervousness, weakness, insomnia, vivid dreaming, nausea, excessive perspiration, loss of appetite, and impairment of memory. These symptoms are often dismissed by the alcoholic as "normal" reactions to an excessive alcohol intake, particularly in the very beginning of the disease. "I overdid it last night," the alcoholic confesses to a nonalcoholic friend, who nods his head in sympathy, having experienced some dreadful hangovers himself.

Most drinkers, of course, are familiar with the hangover. It usually begins when the drinker gets out of bed in the morning. A pounding headache signals the start of a rough day, and the unhappy victim walks into the bathroom, searching for aspirin, Alka Seltzer, or some other remedy to relieve the pain. The creak of the door hurts his head, and the light blinds his eyes. He is thirsty, and no matter how much he drinks, the thirst lingers on. His mouth is cottony dry. The mere thought of alcohol turns his stomach upside down. When he finally makes it through the day, he may swear to himself that he will never drink that much again.

The hangover can be excruciating for the non-alcoholic, but it becomes much worse for the alcoholic in the later stages of his disease. As one expert put it, "[Hangovers] . . . are so extreme for the alcoholic that they really should have a different name. No normal drinker would recognize them as what he has."[1] The source of the physical and mental pain of the alcoholic hangover is, to repeat, the state of hyperactivity in the central nervous system caused by the withdrawal of alcohol. The cells, which are accustomed to the presence of alcohol and dependent on it for energy, stimulation, and sedation, become agitated when it is suddenly not available. The cells' distress is experienced by the alcoholic as the headache, eyeache, dizziness, nausea, and anguish characteristic of the hangover.*

Alcoholics feel physically wretched during a hangover, but they also feel deeply and profoundly ashamed. From past experience, they know better, but they got drunk anyway—Why? Ignorant of the powerful workings of the addiction, the alcoholic can only blame himself. Remorse, self-loathing, and guilt therefore go hand in hand with the throbbing headache and queasy stomach. Some students of alcoholism believe—wrongly—that these emotions are actually responsible for causing the pain of the hangover. "The increasing misery of the hangover is not due to the headache, the nausea, the cold sweats, the chills and fever, or even the shakes," writes psychiatrist Benjamin Karpman, "but to the emotional pain which accompanies them—the guilt, anxiety, self-accusation, the sense of hopelessness and despair.[2]

---

*"Anguish" is an older term than "anxiety" and refers to both mental and physical pain or suffering. "Anxiety" refers only to psychological conflict or tension.

But Karpman has placed the cart before the horse. The alcoholic hangover is not an emotional illness, as he implies, but a very real and very painful physiological disorder.

The increasing misery of the alcoholic hangover is directly caused by the drinker's physical dependence on alcohol. As this goes by and the alcoholic drinks more, and more often, the withdrawal symptoms—experienced in those minutes, hours, or days without a drink—become more severe. He begins to feel shame and remorse when he repeatedly fails in his efforts to stop drinking or control his intake. He cannot make good his intentions to drink as everyone else does, and this personal failure causes great guilt and despair. The alcoholic believes that he should be able to control himself by a sheer force of will. He does not know that the physical addiction is in command of his every thought and action and subverts his persistent efforts to control it.

Alcoholics may swear to themselves, their wives, children, clergymen, or anyone else concerned with their drinking that they will control their intake. But their addiction makes certain that they will drink in spite of their best intentions and heartfelt promises. The alcoholic's most cherished values—his honesty, integrity, self-discipline, even his love for his family—are repeatedly overthrown because he cannot reliably predict or control his own drinking behavior. Any normal human being would feel disgust and self-loathing at this seemingly pathetic inability to exert control and exercise will power; and so does the alcoholic, who may be normal in every respect except his reaction to alcohol.

The alcoholic's guilt, depression, self-loathing, and despair are therefore understandable reactions to a bewildering and mysterious inability to stop the ravages of drinking. Neither the alcoholic nor those around him know that his cells have become abnormal, for the physical dependence and cellular addiction have worked inside him for months or perhaps years, invisible and unnoticed. No wonder the alcoholic believes he is weak-willed and pathetic. No wonder many of the people who observe his behavior believe that he is psychologically unstable, self-destructive, and perhaps suicidal. Without an understanding or knowledge of his addiction, they have no way of knowing that the alcoholic's irrational behavior is beyond his control.

Later Symptoms of Withdrawal. Convulsions, hallucinations, and delirium tremens (DT's) are rare in the early stages of the disease, but are occasionally seen in the middle stages and are more frequently found in the later stages. Late-stage alcoholics who drink heavily for long periods of time are prime candidates for these severe withdrawal symptoms.

Alcoholic convulsions are similar to grand mal epileptic convulsions and involve loss of consciousness and bodily control, extreme rigidity or tenseness, and jerking movements. They may be triggered by a number of physical disorders brought about by the withdrawal of alcohol, including extremely low blood sugar, low levels of certain hormones in the blood, malnutrition, and the accumulation of waste products and toxins in the blood stream.

Hallucinations, like other symptoms of withdrawal, indicate a profound disorder in the central nervous system. They are usually terrifying for the alcoholic as they involve such horror-film ingredients as butcher knives, ghosts, excrement, bloody body parts, ants, bees, lions, and rodents. However, not all hallucinations are frightening and horrible, and sometimes alcoholics are even aware that they are hallucinating.

An elderly man, hospitalized for chronic alcoholism and suffering from frightening hallucinations involving brown furry animals with teeth like nails, was placed in restraints overnight. The next day the nurse found him staring peacefully at the ceiling, clearly enchanted with some happy daydream.

"Mr. Smith," she asked, "are you all right?" He nodded dreamily. "What has happened?" she asked curiously.

"I learned to switch channels," he replied.

Delirium Tremens (DT's), sometimes referred to as "the horrors," are the most dramatic and dangerous expression of withdrawal. Translated directly from Latin, "delirium tremens" means "trembling delirium" or "shaking insanity." The DT's typically begin three to four days after the alcoholic's last drink, when alcohol is completely eliminated from the blood stream, and they usually last anywhere from three to seven agonizing days. Alcoholics who are severely malnourished and have been drinking heavily for prolonged periods are the most common victims, but brain injuries and other traumas or medical complications can aggravate withdrawal and trigger DT's in early- and middle-stage alcoholics.

An alcoholic in DT's is mentally disoriented, hallucinating, and unable to control the movements of his body. Like all the symptoms of acute withdrawal, however, the DT's have any number of outward expressions. Some alcoholics experience violent and terrifying hallucinations, others become aggressive and dangerous, and still others may sweat and shake while concentrating intently on playing a game of cards with a nonexistent deck. As Mark Twain's description in *Huckleberry Finn* so masterfully illustrates, the disorder is completely in control of the victim's body and mind:

I don't know how long I was asleep [Huck Finn confides] but all of a sudden there was an awful scream and I was up. There was pap looking wild, and skipping around every which way and yelling about snakes. He said they was crawling up his legs; and then he would give a jump and scream, and say one had bit him on the cheek—but I couldn't see no snakes. He started to run round and round the cabin, hollering "Take him off! take him off; he's biting me in the neck!" I never see a man look so wild in the eyes. Pretty soon he was all fagged out, and fell down panting; then he rolled over and over wonderful fast, kicking things every which way, and striking and grabbing at the air with his hands, and screaming and saying there was devils a-hold of him. He wore out by and by, and laid still awhile, moaning. Then he laid stiller, and didn't make a sound. I could hear the owls and wolves away off in the woods, and it seemed terrible still. He was laying over by the corner. By and by he raised up part way and listened, with his head to one side. He says, very low: "Tramp—tramp—tramp; that's the dead; tramp—tramp—tramp; they're coming after me, but I won't go. Oh, they're here! don't touch me—don't! hands off—they're cold; let go. Oh, let a poor devil alone!" Then he went down on all fours and crawled off, begging them to let him alone, and he rolled himself up in his blanket and wallowed in under the old pine table, still a-begging; and then he went to crying. . . .

No matter how violent, distracted, or peaceful the alcoholic might seem, the DT's are clearly a sign of deep disturbances in the brain and throughout the body. The condition is so stressful that any other medical complication occurring simultaneously such as gastrointestinal problems, pancreatitis, or heart and liver disease can cause a fatal breakdown in the alcoholic's already seriously overstressed body. In some instances, the trauma of DT's alone may be severe enough to precipitate a massive coronary, brain hemorrhage, or respiratory shutdown, any of which can be fatal.

The mortality rate of untreated patients suffering from DT's is about 20-25 percent, which is estimated to be some forty times higher than the withdrawal fatality rate for heroin addicts. The DT's would undoubtedly kill even more alcoholics if accidents, suicides, or other diseases did not kill them first. Most alcoholics, however, either recover or die from their disease before reaching this most severe and life-threatening stage of alcoholism.

The DT's could be virtually eliminated if all alcoholics received adequate medical treatment during acute withdrawal. The incidence of DT's has already been significantly reduced as more and more alcoholics receive medical care in in-patient treatment centers.

The Protracted Withdrawal Syndrome

Even if the alcoholic is able to endure the acute withdrawal syndrome without taking a drink to relieve his anguish, his troubles are not over. The majority of alcoholics continue to be anxious, depressed, nervous, and fearful long after they stop drinking. Alcoholics abstinent for months and even years may complain of insomnia, depression, agitation, moodiness, and an overwhelming desire for alcohol. Because so many alcoholics experience these symptoms to some degree, many people conclude that the alcoholic is and always has been psychologically troubled. Experts label those alcoholics who suffer recurring psychological or emotional problems "neurotic," "anxiety prone," or simply "immature." These alcoholics are sometimes put on tranquilizers or sedatives in hope of alleviating their mental suffering. Those who finally break down and drink, no longer able to endure life without alcohol, may be considered hopelessly depressed or morbidly suicidal.

The sober "recovering" alcoholic is baffled by his

continuing depression and anxiety, and he, too, may conclude that his problems are primarily psychological. His hopelessness and despair are overwhelming, and he is haunted by questions which already appear to be answered in the affirmative: "Am I simply an emotionally unstable person who drinks to ease my problems? Will I always return to drinking because I am so weak and psychologically sick?" When his problems persist, the sober alcoholic is frustrated and afraid. He may very well believe that he was better off when he was drinking, for alcohol always seemed to ease his problems. His options appear to be few, and his future precarious.

Yet the alcoholic's persistent problems are not caused by any inherent psychological flaws or emotional weaknesses but by the physical disease itself. The depression and anxiety are actually long-term (or protracted) withdrawal symptoms, and they indicate that the cells are still suffering from the damage caused by alcohol. The healing process is not automatically completed when the alcoholic stops drinking. Alcohol has created widespread destruction throughout the body, and the cells need time to heal. They also need help if the healing process is to be rapid and complete.

The major causes of the protracted withdrawal syndrome are malnutrition, hypoglycemia, autonomic nervous system dysfunctions, cortical atrophy, and brain amine depletion. Each of these physiological abnormalities needs to be understood in the context of alcoholism.

Malnutrition. All alcoholics are malnourished to some extent because excessive alcohol intake interferes with the body's ability to absorb and use various nutrients regardless of what the alcoholic may be eating. The cells, of course, are dependent on an adequate supply of nutrients to perform their everyday functions, heal themselves, and create new cells.

Alcohol's massive assault on the structure and functioning of the alcoholic's cells cannot be reversed

73

just by removing alcohol from the body—abstinence alone does not make malnourished cells healthy again. The cells need vitamins, minerals, amino acids, proteins, fats, and carbohydrates, and they need them in therapeutic amounts and proportions. Without an adequate supply of these nutrients, the cells cannot get on with the long process of repairing the damage done by excessive drinking.

Most recovering alcoholics do not even know that they are suffering from nutritional damage, and even if informed about their condition, they probably do not realize that a balanced diet and nutritional supplements will help them make a rapid and complete recovery. As discussed above, they are more likely to suppose that their psychological distress is caused by psychological problems—a misconcepton widely shared by society and by most therapists as well.

Another aspect of malnutrition which is widely misunderstood and overlooked is *hypoglycemia*, or chronic low blood sugar. This condition, which is prevalent in both early- and late-stage alcoholics, is usually caused by diseases or disorders in the liver or endocrine glands which affect the body's ability to store and release blood sugar or glucose. Alcoholics have various malfunctions in liver enzyme activities which may result in a decreased ability to convert glycogen into glucose.* A malfunction in the activity of the endocrine glands may also be involved.

When the blood sugar drops to abnormally low levels, the alcoholic experiences symptoms of fatigue, headache, sleepiness, forgetfulness, inability to concentrate, moodiness, anxiety, depression, hunger, and shakiness. Alcohol immediately brings the blood sugar level up and makes the symptoms disappear. After one or two drinks, the hypoglycemic feels remarkably better. His headaches and sleepiness are gone, and the mental

---

*See chapter 3 for a full discussion of liver enzyme malfunctions.

confusion, depression and anxiety miraculously fade away.

Alcohol is thus an attractive first aid for hypoglycemia, but it is poor therapy because it triggers a series of chemical changes which soon make the blood sugar level drop like a rock once again. As the blood sugar level crashes down, the symptoms of hypoglycemia return with a vengeance—and a reinforcement: the desire for alcohol to relieve the symptoms.

Hypoglycemia is a chronic condition. The symptoms do not simply disappear when the alcoholic stops drinking, and he must therefore carefully regulate his sugar intake to control the level of glucose in his blood. This can be accomplished through simple dietary measures.†

Tragically, most alcoholics are not aware of this condition or its significance. Most treatment programs ignore or compromise the hypoglycemic diet and thus do little or nothing to enlighten their patients. Without an adjustment in sugar intake, the alcoholic's feelings of depression and anxiety may continue indefinitely, and he may never escape the desire for a drink to relieve his "psychological" symptoms.

There are other areas in which the healing process will be blocked or slowed down if malnutrition and hypoglycemia are not recognized and treated. In particular, certain dysfunctions related to central nervous system damage, including autonomic nervous system dysfunction, cortical atrophy, and brain amine depletion, may continue.

Autonomic Nervous System (ANS) Dysfunction. Large amounts of alcohol taken over a prolonged period of time can upset the orderly workings of the ANS,[3] which is responsible for overseeing the work of the involuntary glands, the cardiac muscle, and the smooth muscles such as those of the digestive system, the

----

†See Appendixes B (Guidelines for a Hypoglycemic Diet) and C (A Sample Hypoglycemic Diet and Snacks).

respiratory system, and the skin. Particularly during the first months of sobriety, the alcoholic may show signs of tremor, excess perspiration, and rapid pulse and heart rates—all signs of malfunctioning in the autonomic nervous system. These disturbances are found in lesser degrees in alcoholics abstinent for up to two years, and they lessen further as sobriety lengthens. As in the treatment of hypoglycemia, comprehensive nutritional therapy will promote more rapid healing of the ANS and an end to the alcoholic's continued suffering.

Cortical Atrophy. Approximately half of late-stage alcoholics experience measurable deterioration of function in the cortex, the layer of gray matter blanketing the two hemispheres of the brain.[4] The cortex is involved in a number of functions, including the major senses of sight, hearing, touch, taste, and smell, the direction of conscious movements of the body, reasoning, and memory. Damage to one or more of these functions may be permanent, but most alcoholics with cortical damage will gradually recover normal functioning as the period of sobriety lengthens and the body is allowed to heal itself. Nutritional therapy is once again a crucial element in ensuring improvement and promoting rapid recovery.

Brain Amine Depletion. In alcoholics, the levels of at least two brain amines—serotonin and norepinephrine—are significantly lower in the protracted withdrawal period, apparently contributing to the alcoholic's continuing depression, anxiety, tension, and irritability.[5] Brain amines are the substances responsible for transmitting chemical messages from one brain cell to another and regulating various emotional states. The amines usually return to normal activity after several weeks or months of sobriety, although insomnia and nightmares may persist for years. A decrease in serotonin, in particular, seems to be at least partially responsible for

76

persistent sleep disturbances. Studies have shown a connection between decreases in serotonin, insomnia, and disruptions of deep (stage IV) sleep.[6] With comprehensive nutritional therapy, however, sleep disturbances are rarely seen after the first weeks of sobriety.[7]

Craving

Craving is the overwhelming need for a drink. Like everything else in alcoholism, craving is progressive. During the early stages of the disease, craving is related to the benefits the alcoholic experiences from drinking—the alcoholic wants to drink because drinking makes him feel so good. In the middle stages of the disease, craving becomes a need—the alcoholic needs to drink because his cells are physically dependent on alcohol. In the deteriorative stages of the disease, the alcoholic drinks more directly for the purpose of relieving the psychological and physiological distress of withdrawal. Craving has gradually evolved into an overpowering obsession—the alcoholic craves alcohol because it is the most effective remedy for the pain he feels when he stops drinking.

Early in the disease the alcoholic can usually control his craving for alcohol, but since there are so few penalties associated with drinking and so many benefits, he feels no need for control. As tolerance increases and physical dependence sets in, the alcoholic gradually loses psychological control over his physiological need for alcohol. Finally, will power, self-restraint, and the ability to say "no" have no power over alcoholic craving. The physical need for alcohol overshadows everything else in the alcoholic's life.

A great controversy surrounds this experience of craving. Most experts agree that alcoholics experience a physical need for alcohol whenever their alcohol intake is delayed during a drinking bout. This physical need is caused by the acute withdrawal symptoms—the alcoholic's great physical distress when his BAL starts to drop. In an effort to forestall these painful symptoms, the alcoholic keeps on drinking.

Disagreement prevails, however, over whether the sober alcoholic actually needs a drink in between drinking bouts, or just thinks he does. Withdrawal symptoms are no longer present, many experts insist, and the alcoholic therefore is motivated only by a psychological need or desire to drink again. Even E. M. Jellinek, the renowned authority on alcoholism and author of *The Disease Concept of Alcoholism*, once wrote, "[The alcoholic's continuing complaints]... seem to be... indications of insufficient adaptation on the symbolic level to an alcohol-free life."[8]

Jellinek appears to be saying that the alcoholic feels sorry for himself because he can no longer drink and that his problems at this point are therefore basically psychological. But, as has been stressed, most of the alcoholic's problems are caused by physiological factors. Months or years after his last drink, the alcoholic may experience physical withdrawal symptoms, and his craving for alcohol is a true physiological need to relieve these symptoms. The abstinent alcoholic will continue to suffer from protracted withdrawal symptoms until the healing process is complete. Again, without nutritional therapy he may never fully recover.

Loss of Control

As the alcoholic progressively loses control over his drinking, he is no longer able to restrict it to socially and culturally accepted times and places. He often drinks more than he intended, and the drinking continues despite extremely punishing consequences. He may drink in the morning, at lunch, in the middle of the night; he may drink in the car, the bathroom, the garage, or the closet as well as the tavern. His drinking behavior can no longer be disguised as normal or even heavy drinking. His inability to stop drinking—despite his firm resolution that he will stop after one or two—is striking confirmation that he is physically addicted to alcohol.

The alcoholic loses control over his drinking because his tolerance decreases and the withdrawal symptoms increase. The alcoholic's tolerance, which was so high in the early stages of the disease, begins to decrease because his cells have been damaged and can no longer tolerate large amounts of alcohol. While tolerance is lessening, the withdrawal symptoms are increasing in severity. The alcoholic is now in the dangerous position of needing to drink because he suffers terribly when he stops drinking but being unable to handle the high levels of alcohol needed to relieve the symptoms. He has also lost the ability to judge accurately how much alcohol his body can handle. As a result, he often overmedicates himself with alcohol, drinking to the point where he either loses consciousness or becomes so violently ill that he is forced to stop drinking.

Loss of control does not happen all of a sudden, nor is it always characterized by the alcoholic's drinking everything in sight. Loss of control occurs gradually and is sometimes evident in the early stages of the disease when the alcoholic occasionally overdrinks his tolerance. The effects of overdrinking are extremely unpleasant, however, and the early-stage alcoholic will make every attempt to drink within his tolerance level. At this point in the disease, he is usually able to exert considerable control over his drinking and thus can usually avoid the penalties.

As alcoholism progresses, the episodes of uncontrolled drinking become more frequent and severe. The middle- or late-stage alcoholic may start drinking in the morning in an attempt to alleviate the tremors in his hands, the queasiness in his belly, and the ache in his head. The first drink works quickly, and the second drink makes him feel almost normal. Soon, however, his blood alcohol level begins to descend as the alcohol is gradually broken down and eliminated, the acetaldehyde level builds up, and the alcoholic starts feeling jittery again. He throws down another drink and then another in an attempt to forestall his agitation and anxiety. Some alcoholics may never drink in the early morning or never after dinner, but the progression will still be there. A drink or two may be "necessary" at lunch. Lunch may stretch out until midafternoon. For the rest of the workday, the alcoholic may sip from a bottle hidden in his desk. He may have a drink as soon as he gets home, and his predinner drinks may step up in number.

This cycle of drinking is, in fact, an effort to relieve the impending withdrawal symptoms, and it may go on for some time. Healthier alcoholics can drink for days or even weeks, precariously balancing the benefits of drinking with the increasing penalties of withdrawal. Severely malnourished alcoholics whose tolerance for alcohol has decreased significantly or alcoholics with liver disease or gastritis may only be able to put off the penalties for a few hours or perhaps a day or two of drinking.

Soon enough, more alcohol must be drunk to compete with the rate at which alcohol is being eliminated. It is a race against time—a losing race. At some point, alcohol is no longer capable of neutralizing the increasing anguish, tremors, and nausea, and the alcoholic is forced to stop drinking because he passes out or becomes acutely ill. The alcoholic who drinks to this extreme has clearly lost control.

6

The Late, Deteriorative Stage of Alcoholism

Among all sources of disease, alcohol stands pre-eminent as a destroyer. . . . This pestilent principle generally seeks for asylum where it may practice its deadliest deeds in some important and vital organ of the body. It sometimes makes the brain more particularly the seat of its venom, and victim of its cruelties. At another time, it hides itself in the inmost recess of the heart, or coils around it like a serpent; now it fixes upon the lungs; now upon the kidneys, upon the liver, the bladder, the pancreas, the intestines or the skin. It can agitate the heart until it throbs and bursts, or it can reduce pulsation until it becomes impalpable. It can distract the head until the brain sweats blood, and horrified reason flies away and leaves the man a maniac or a madman. . . . I never knew a person become insane who was not in the habit of taking a portion of alcohol daily.

Benjamin Parsons, an English
clergyman, in *Anti-Bacchus:
An Essay on the Crimes, Diseases,
and Other Evils Connected with the
Use of Intoxicating Drinks, 1840*

Once again, although the distinction between the middle and late stages of alcoholism is somewhat arbitrary, it can be identified as that point at which symptoms associated with adaptation to alcohol are gradually overcome by symptoms that reflect increasing toxicity and damage to body organs and systems. The alcoholic's tolerance to alcohol is progressively lessening because of cell damage in the liver and central nervous system, and his withdrawal symptoms are increasing in severity. The late-stage alcoholic spends most of his time drinking, since otherwise his agony is excruciating.

When most people think of an alcoholic, they think of him in this final stage of the disease: destitute, deathly ill, mentally confused, and living only for alcohol. Yet his deterioration began long before this last stage, in most cases years before any physical damage became apparent. Deterioration, in fact, began in the early and middle stages of the disease, as described in chapters 4 and 5, when the alcoholic's cells adapted to alcohol, allowing it into the body in ever larger doses. It progressed gradually as the cells became physically dependent on alcohol, until finally there were so many alterations in normal functioning that the disease could no longer remain hidden and emerged full-blown.

During the late stages of alcoholism, the alcoholic's mental and physical health are seriously deteriorated. Damage to vital organs saps the alcoholic's physical strength; resistance to disease and infection is lowered; mental stability is shaken and precarious. The late-stage alcoholic is so ravaged by his disease that he cannot even understand that alcohol is destroying him. He is only aware that alcohol offers quick and miraculous relief from the constant agony, mental confusion, and emotional turmoil. Alcohol, his deadly poison, is also his necessary medicine.

If the alcoholic continues to drink, alcohol will kill him in one way or another. Estimates vary, but according to one source, one-third of alcoholic deaths are from suicides or accidents such as drownings, fires from passing out with a lighted cigarette, head injuries from falling, accidental poisoning, or car crashes.[1] Those who survive these hazards are destroyed by direct and massive damage to body organs and systems. It is of interest that only 14 percent of the deaths actually caused by alcoholism are so labelled.

Most statistics on deaths caused by alcoholism are based on middle- and late-stage alcoholics who show some physical deterioration or damage from drinking. The early-stage alcoholic is rarely diagnosed as such, and thus death at that stage is rarely attributed to alcoholism. If early-stage alcoholics were accurately represented in alcoholism death statistics, the leading cause of death would probably be accidents or suicides rather than medical complications. The tragedy of the disease is revealed in these statistics, for alcoholics too often die of their disease before it is diagnosed.

Causes of Death in a Group of Alcoholics

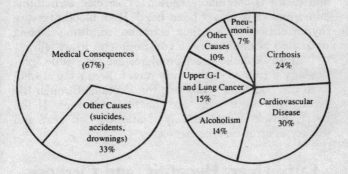

From W. Schmidt and R. E. Popham, unpublished data, "Deaths in 1823 Male Alcoholics, Corrected for the Expected Mortality in Each Subgroup" (1978)

As the disease progresses into the final stages, alcohol destroys in a scattergun approach, hitting the heart, liver, brain, stomach, lungs, kidneys, and pancreas. The alcoholic dies when one specific organ stops functioning, but every vital organ suffers massive damage. The major medical consequences of alcoholic drinking include heart failure, liver disease, gastrointestinal disorders, cancer, respiratory tract disease, pancreatitis, and malnutrition.

Heart Failure

Heart failure is a major cause of death in alcoholism. High levels of alcohol and acetaldehyde apparently act directly on the cell membranes in the heart muscle (myocardium), altering their shape and functioning. Various enzymes then leak from the cells, cell mitochondria are damaged, and the cells are slowly infiltrated with fat. The symptoms of alcoholic cardiomyopathy (disease of the heart muscle) are heart palpitations and labored or difficult breathing. Neural and chemical mechanisms that regulate the heart may be overcome, and death is commonly caused by cardiac arrhythmia (abnormal variations of heart beat). High blood pressure (hypertension) is another common condition among untreated alcoholics and a contributor to heart failure.

Most alcoholic heart problems are reversible, particularly if treated in the early stages. Removing alcohol from the body and protecting the alcoholic through the acute withdrawal stage are the first priorities. If the heart muscle is extensively damaged, bed rest and dietary control may be necessary.

Fatty Liver, Hepatitis, and Cirrhosis

The body needs fuel to continue functioning, and its major fuel sources are carbohydrates and fat. The liver is the major organ for converting these substances into energy. When alcohol is in the body, however, the liver has a choice. It can either use alcohol or the fat and carbohydrates for fuel. Because alcohol requires less time and effort to oxidize than these other sources of fuel, and the calories available from its breakdown provide a rich and potent energy "kick," the choice is quickly made. The liver uses the alcohol as a fuel, the carbohydrates are stored as glycogen or converted to fat, and the fat is kept in storage.

Thus, whenever alcohol is in the body, the liver uses it for fuel rather than the more difficult and time-consuming fat. This substitution of alcohol for fat as a fuel is not restricted to the alcoholic but, in fact, occurs in everyone who drinks a significant amount of alcohol. The nonalcoholic drinker, however, usually drinks only for short periods, with relatively long periods of abstention in between. When there is no alcohol in the body, the fat is pulled out of storage and converted by the liver into energy to fulfill the body's needs. Alcoholics, on the other hand, keep a fairly constant supply of alcohol in the liver, and as a result, fat accumulates.

Alcohol contributes to the buildup of fat in the liver in another major and potentially disastrous way. Large amounts of alcohol trigger various hormonal discharges which mobilize the fat stored and deposited in other body tissues and move it toward the liver, which must then make room to store it. Surplus fat also circulates in the blood stream as triglycerides.

As the fat accumulates, it begins to crowd the highly specialized liver cells, many of which suffocate and die. This condition is termed *fatty infiltration of the liver*. As more and more liver cells are injured, the fatty deposits enlarge, causing the liver to swell. A healthy liver is normally neatly tucked away behind the rib cage on the right side and cannot be felt at all. But as the fat and swelling increase, the inflamed liver can be felt by pressing up under the bottom rib. In advanced cases, the swelling can extend down to the pelvis on the right side. The typical person with a severe case of alcoholic fatty liver has been drinking heavily for weeks or months, has no appetite, and suffers from nausea and jaundice.

In some alcoholics, large numbers of cells are sick and begin to die, and the liver becomes inflamed, swollen, and extremely tender. This condition is known as *alcoholic hepatitis*. The alcoholic with hepatitis is nauseated, feverish, jaundiced, and complains of abdominal pain. Both fatty liver and hepatitis are reversible with abstinence from alcohol and good nutrition to promote healing. But if the alcoholic continues to drink, so many of his liver cells may be destroyed that scar tissue begins to form, signifying the condition known as *cirrhosis* of the liver.[2] Cirrhosis occurs in an estimated 8 percent of alcoholics, about seven times as often as in nonalcoholics.

A cirrhotic liver is a plugged up liver, something like a drain that is clogged. Blood cannot flow smoothly through the congested organ; it backs up and is gradually saturated with toxic materials. As the poisoned blood flow reaches the brain, the cells become poisoned and sick, profoundly affecting the alcoholic's behavior and emotions. The toxic alcoholic is confused, his thought processes jumbled and rambling, and memory and judgment muddled. Even his balance and equilibrium may be affected.

As the scar tissue in the liver accumulates and ages, it also constricts, choking the blood vessels and cutting off the blood supply to the remaining liver cells, which causes further cell death. If the alcoholic continues to drink, the combined effects of fatty liver, hepatitis, and cirrhosis have additional serious consequences. When the blood can no longer circulate freely through the congested liver, the pressure created causes the small blood vessels in the head, face, and chest to rupture, resulting in tiny, spiderlike patterns of broken blood vessels called *spider angioma*.

As the body's blood vessels become constricted, alternate routes to the heart must be found. One route is through the thin-walled and delicate veins of the esophagus. The increased blood flow through these veins can cause them to dilate and, like a bicycle tire blown up with too much air, rupture and hemorrhage. Bleeding from the esophageal vessels (or varices) is evident when the alcoholic vomits up fresh blood. These hemorrhages are obviously dangerous and one of the major causes of death of cirrhosis victims.

Ascites is another complication of the pressure created by a cirrhotic liver. Specifically, ascites is a symptom of pressure in the lymphatic system. When the pressure grows too great, lymph leaks out of the vessels, accumulating in the abdomen, which then swells. Ascites is sometimes mistaken for the common and relatively harmless beer belly, but a swollen stomach in a heavy drinker should be a clear warning of serious trouble in the liver.

Many other serious and sometimes fatal complications occur as a result of cirrhosis. Because so many of its cells are dead or injured, the liver's ability to detoxify poisons is greatly reduced, and potentially dangerous chemicals build up in the blood stream. One of these is ammonia, which can cause personality changes, lethargy, coma, and death. Bilirubin is another chemical which builds up in the blood when the liver is plugged up with scar tissue. This orange bile pigment is a breakdown product of hemoglobin, and its accumulation causes yellowing of the skin, or jaundice.

As liver damage progresses, other essential chemical and hormonal substances are produced at a slower rate because the liver is simply not functioning normally. Among these is prothrombin, an ingredient necessary for clotting blood. As the prothrombin level decreases, the alcoholic may bruise easily and bleed excessively from a small cut or scratch. He may have bleeding gums, frequent and severe nosebleeds, or bleeding under the skin. If the prothrombin level gets too low, the alcoholic is in danger of dying from internal hemorrhage.

Up to the point of scar tissue development, the liver has extraordinary regenerative powers, and amazing transformations take place when the liver is given proper food and nutrients, rest, and no alcohol. The body slowly eliminates the accumulated fatty tissue, the liver rebuilds itself, the blood is cleansed of its impurities, and the chemical balance in the brain is gradually restored.

If the alcoholic continues to drink and if scar tissue begins to form, however, the blood vessels will be gradually choked off and the liver cells will sicken and die until the formerly mighty and complex factory of the liver is reduced to a decrepit, fragile structure clogged with poisons, wastes, and dead cells and incapable of sustaining life.

Gastrointestinal Disorders

The stomach is the site of astonishingly powerful chemical reactions which can reduce substances as difficult to digest as fish bones, toothpicks, and gristle to a soft mush which is then easily transported through the small intestines and eliminated from the body. Something has to protect the stomach from digesting itself in this process, however, and this role belongs to the mucous membrane which lines the stomach and to a layer of specialized cells directly beneath the mucous membrane. One of the most important parts of this protective barrier is the cell membrane which contains a layer of fats and proteins tightly cemented together to prevent leakage of digestive juices. This multilayered barrier allows the digestive enzymes to do their violent work while protecting the soft stomach walls from being dissolved in the process.

In the early- and middle-stage alcoholic, alcohol sabotages this intricate protective system by assaulting the fat and protein layer of the membranes and weakening the tight links between the cells. Digestive juices may now leak through the cells and onto the membranes. The lining of the stomach may then become seriously inflamed, a condition known as *gastritis*. Gastritis can be severe enough to cause bleeding, and its symptoms include indigestion, bloating, nausea, headache, and abnormal increase or decrease in appetite. Ironically, the best temporary first aid for gastritis is alcohol. Researchers have graphically depicted the amazing transformation of a stomach raw and inflamed after a prolonged drinking bout to a "normal" stomach after just one or two drinks.[3] Taken in large enough amounts, however, alcohol will once again aggravate the inflammation.

Ulcers are also very common during the high tolerance phases of early- and middle-stage alcoholism and less frequent in the late stages of the disease when tolerance is lowered. Ulceration corresponds with an increased secretion of hydrochloric acid in the early- and middle-stage alcoholic. Late-stage alcoholics have lowered levels of hydrochloric acid secretion.

Respiratory Tract Diseases

In general, alcoholism causes damage to the lungs by interfering with the body's normal defense mechanisms and thereby making the alcoholic susceptible to respiratory infection and injury. Large doses of alcohol taken over long periods of time may block the formation of new cells, prevent living cells from destroying bacteria, and delay the lung's ability to eliminate inhaled particles. This interference with normal functioning can lead to infections, tuberculosis, chronic bronchitis, emphysema, and lung abscess. The acute inflammation or infection of the lung (pneumonia) is a frequent cause of death for late-stage alcoholics. One study reported that death rates from pneumonia were three times higher for alcoholic men than for the general population and seven times higher for alcoholic women.[4]

Cancer

The clinical association of long-term ingestion of large amounts of alcoholic beverages (chronic alcoholism) with a variety of cancers is known to most cancer epidemiologists but is not widely recognized in the medical profession.[5]

Alcohol is not a widely accepted cancer-causing agent, but there are strong indications that large amounts of alcohol taken over a prolonged period of time definitely contribute to or aggravate cancers throughout the body. Alcoholics appear to have an increased risk of head and neck, esophageal, lung, and liver cancers. In each of these cancers, alcohol probably acts in a different way, sometimes directly affecting the cells, other times indirectly increasing the cells' susceptibility to cancer. There are a number of ways alcohol appears to contribute to cancer:

- By directly irritating the cells, thus targeting an area which may then be more vulnerable to cancer.
- By damaging the liver so that the ability to break down and neutralize poisonous substances is greatly reduced. The accumulation of these substances in the blood may directly irritate the cells, increasing the likelihood of cancer. The common coexistence of alcoholic cirrhosis and liver tumors provides strong evi-

dence that advanced alcoholism is related to cancer in the liver. However, it is probably the cirrhosis, not alcohol itself, that is directly responsible for an increased risk of liver cancer.

- By causing nutritional deficiencies which may further weaken the cells' ability to withstand the toxic effects of large amounts of alcohol.
- By providing a vehicle for the chemical additives (congeners) which give alcoholic beverages their distinctive taste, smell, and color and which may be cancer-causing agents.
- By interacting with tobacco and increasing the risks of each taken separately. The effect may be synergistic, or multiplied, and therefore the risk of drinking and smoking at the same time may be much higher than that associated with taking either alone.
- By inhibiting salivation and thus interfering with the body's normal rinsing mechanisms. For alcoholics who are also heavy cigarette smokers, a buildup of tars in the saliva may contribute to the development of cancers of the head, neck, and esophagus.

Pancreatitis

Large and continuous doses of alcohol apparently injure the pancreas, causing it to activate and release certain digestive enzymes which, in turn, aggravate the inflammation of this vital gland located behind the stomach and liver. In extreme cases, the digestive enzymes may actually begin to digest the pancreas.

Pancreatitis usually develops after five to fifteen years of heavy drinking and is characterized by severe pain in the upper abdomen, often radiating to the back and lower chest, nausea, vomiting, and constipation. Abstinence dramatically reduces the frequency and severity of the attacks.

Malnutrition

All alcoholics suffer from malnutrition to some degree. A number of factors work together to make this condition almost synonymous with alcoholism. Large doses of alcohol interfere with digestion and passage of nutrients from the intestines into the bloodstream. The alcoholic's liver has a decreased ability to convert and release nutrients and make them available throughout the body. Without adequate nutrients, the cells, already weakened by long exposures to alcohol's toxic effects, are not able to create bone, tissue, blood, or energy. The sick and injured cells thus do not have the resources to repair themselves, and damage continues unchecked.

Even the alcoholic's earliest psychological and social problems stem from or are aggravated by nutritional deficiencies. For example, a thiamine deficiency (extremely common in alcoholics) can cause loss of mental alertness, easy fatigue, loss of appetite, irritability, and emotional instability. If the deficiency is allowed to continue, more severe mental confusion and loss of memory may develop.

In the later stages of alcoholism, the alcoholic is often so sick that he cannot eat, thus aggravating the already serious nutritional deficiencies. Massive vitamin or mineral deficiencies caused by long and heavy drinking may result in several unusual diseases of the central nervous system, including polyneuropathy, Wernicke's encephalopathy, Korsakoff's psychosis, and amblyopia.

Polyneuropathy is a nutritional disorder generally associated with deficiencies of the B complex vitamins—including thiamine (B_1), pantothenic acid, nicotinic acid, and pyridoxine (B_6)—which weaken and eventually damage the peripheral nerves outside the brain and spinal cord. These nerves, which are similar to thin, elongated wires, carry electrical/chemical impulses which instruct the legs, arms, and torso to lift, move, run, walk, or feel warmth, cold, pain, and pressure. The strength of the current in the nerve depends on adequate food and nutrients for its power source. When the nerves are deprived of nutrients, the power of the sensory and motor impulses diminishes and weakens, and the nerves gradually lose their ability to transmit sensory and motor signals.

The first indications of polyneuropathy are numbness and tingling sensations ("pins and needles") in the extremities, usually the toes or fingers. As the condition progresses, the sensations occur higher in the limbs, affecting hands and arms, feet and legs. Polyneuropathy is reversible if arrested early enough. If the alcoholic stops drinking and continues to abstain from alcohol, and if he pays careful attention to his diet and vitamin and mineral intake (particularly the B vitamins), the nerves will heal themselves fairly quickly. If, however, the alcoholic continues to drink and malnutrition progresses unchecked, there will come a time when the damage is permanent and irreversible. Muscle tone will be lost, and the muscles will atrophy. Pain may be excruciating. Late-stage alcoholics with irreversible polyneuropathy may be able to walk only clumsily if at all.

Wernicke's encephalopathy, named after a nineteenth-century German psychiatrist and brain specialist, is a rare disease usually produced by a severe deficiency in Vitamin B_1 (thiamine). The disease is marked by a rapid onset of headaches, double vision, abnormal eye movements, the tingling sensations and numbness associated with polyneuropathy, muscular incoordination, stupor, and brain hemorrhage. The condition is also frequently accompanied by the confusion, agitation, and hallucinations seen in delirium tremens. In fact, Wernicke's encephalopathy is sometimes a precursor of the DT's.

Until forty years ago, the prognosis invariably was death, but after the B vitamins were synthesized and readily available, significant improvement in the condition became possible and the symptoms are now largely reversible if treated promptly. Immediate treatment is essential, however, because the condition swiftly progresses into the generally irreversible mental disorder called "Korsakoff's psychosis."

Korsakoff's psychosis, first described in 1890 by the Russian psychiatrist Sergei Sergeyevich Korsakoff, is caused, in part, by vitamin B_1 deficiencies, and it generally results in irreversible brain damage. The disorder has several striking characteristics, including hallucinations, the loss of short-term memory, and the consequent fabrication of stories to fill in the gaps (termed "confabulation"). The victim is often able to remember past events but is thoroughly confused as to present or recent events such as where he is, why he happens to be there, what he has just eaten, or who may be sitting next to him.

Amblyopia, another rare disease, occurs in approximately one in two hundred hospitalized alcoholics. It is characterized by progressive blurring or dimness of vision and, in some cases, difficulty in distinguishing green from red. Although the specific nutritional deficiency responsible for this condition has not been identified, amblyopia is readily reversible with improved nutrition and, specifically, large doses of the B vitamins.

Now that the early, middle and late stages of the disease have been described from a technical standpoint, the alcoholic himself must be described. What are the psychological symptoms that he experiences as he progresses from the early to the late stages, and what are his reactions to these symptoms? Most important, why does he continue to drink when drinking is slowly but surely destroying him?

7

The Alcoholic

"Why are you drinking?" demanded the little prince.
"So that I may forget," replied the tippler.
"Forget what?" inquired the little prince, who al-
ready was sorry for him.
"Forget that I am ashamed," the tippler confessed,
hanging his head.
"Ashamed of what?" insisted the little prince, who
wanted to help him.
"Ashamed of drinking!" The tippler brought his speech
to an end, and shut himself up in an impregnable
silence.

Antoine de Saint-Exupéry,
The Little Prince

Once the disease of alcoholism is understood, the
only remaining mystery is the victim—why does the
alcoholic continue to drink after it is evident that drinking is destroying him?

The answer is surprisingly simple: At every stage
the disease itself prevents the alcoholic from realizing
that he is addicted to alcohol. In the earliest stage,
when the cells are adapting and tolerance is gradually
increasing, the alcoholic does not consider giving up
alcohol because nothing indicates that he is sick, and no
one else suspects that he might be. In the middle
stages when his cells have become firmly dependent on

alcohol for functioning, he may be aware that he needs alcohol more often and in greater quantities, but he does not know why. He does not know that his cells have been altered, nor does he know that his physical reaction to alcohol is drastically different from the nonalcoholic's. He only knows that when he stops drinking, he suffers, and so his first priority is to get alcohol back in his system.

As the alcoholic drinks more and more often, alcohol's toxic effects disrupt the brain's chemical and electrical balances, causing profound psychological and emotional disturbances. The middle- and late-stage alcoholic is frequently irrational, deluded, and incapable of understanding what is happening inside him. He cannot see himself as others see him. His actions, thoughts, and emotions are warped by alcohol; his behavior is governed by the addiction.

To everyone else it may appear that the alcoholic is somehow responsible for his disease, because he ignores all warnings and continues to drink. But—and this is a key to understanding alcoholism—he is already an alcoholic when his behavior and psychological stability first begin to deteriorate. The physical disease is already well-established by the time the alcoholic begins to act like an alcoholic. In fact, the disease itself is responsible for most of the alcoholic's psychological problems, and as it progresses, the alcoholic's behavior becomes more bizarre and his psychological problems more profound.

Because the physical damage is not evident until the later stages of the disease when the alcoholic is clearly addicted and can no longer reliably control his drinking, it is critically important that the early psychological and behavioral symptoms of alcoholism be recognized for what they are: the signs of an already established disease. Alcoholics should not have to wait until their lives are nearly destroyed by alcohol before their disease is recognized; they can be diagnosed in the early stages of the disease. An alcoholism specialist who knows what to look for and who understands that psychological and emotional problems are among the first symptoms of underlying alcoholism can make an accurate diagnosis after careful examination. A family history of alcoholism is one clue; marital difficulties, problems at work, recurring bouts of depression and anxiety, and changing drinking patterns are additional clues. A classic symptom of alcoholic drinking is a refusal to acknowledge or admit a drinking problem. The alcoholic will deny or rationalize his drinking behavior because he is unaware of the addiction, believing that his drinking is merely a response to serious life problems.

The alcoholic's interaction with others can also provide telling clues. If the spouse is worried; if a parent is frequently too busy to play with his children or constantly irritated by their demands; if he would rather go drinking than stay at home; if he makes new friends who happen to be heavy drinkers; if he keeps a bottle in the office so that he and his friends can celebrate whenever the mood hits them—all these behaviors raise suspicions of alcoholism.

The alcoholic and others around him, however, usually have a difficult time determining whether alcoholism is at the root of his growing problems. In the later stages of the disease, when addiction is obvious and withdrawal symptoms provide an undeniable sign of physical dependence, the diagnosis is much easier to make. But in the early stages, alcoholic drinking can easily be confused with normal or problem drinking behavior. Simply because a man argues with his wife, stomps out of the house, and gets drunk at the corner tavern does not mean that he is an alcoholic. Marital problems and job difficulties are not sufficient by themselves to indicate alcoholism. But add personality changes and a growing preoccupation with alcohol, and alcoholism is a very likely explanation.

Perhaps the strongest clue of all is the disease's progression. Alcoholism does not do a little damage and then suddenly stop its attack. If the alcoholic continues to drink, he will not be able to reverse his psychological problems; they will only get worse. He will be able to drink in control for only a temporary period; inevitably, alcohol will control him. He will drink more, and more often, in spite of the fact that alcohol is threatening his marriage, career, and health.

Every alcoholic, of course, experiences a slightly different progression of overt symptoms, and not every alcoholic experiences all symptoms. The "typical" alcoholic is therefore a summary of all, not necessarily a description of any individual alcoholic. Given that warning, a description follows of a "typical" progression of symptoms from the early stage through the middle stage and into the final stage of alcoholism.

The Early Stages

Jack is a 45-year-old engineer, popular with his friends and loved by his family. He has four children, lives in a comfortable suburban home, and his favorite hobbies are golf and gardening.

Jack never drinks alone during the day, but at 5:00 p.m. sharp, he sits down in front of the TV and drinks 3 or 4 straight Scotches. He allows nothing to interfere with his "cocktail hour." He knows he drinks a lot, but many of his friends also drink heavily, and nobody seems to be worried about them. Besides, he never lets his drinking interfere with his job or family life, he rarely gets drunk, and alcohol always, without fail, makes him feel better.

The early alcoholic typically enjoys drinking, drinks whenever alcohol is offered, and often seeks out the drinking occasion. An afternoon baseball game may be organized with baseball as the secondary motive and drinking during the game or at a tavern after the game the primary motive. Drinking is fun, socially satisfying, and an important part of the early alcoholic's life.

Many nonalcoholics also drink whenever they have the chance; so the early alcoholic's drinking does not appear unusual or abnormal. Yet even in this early stage, there are symptoms which create suspicion of alcoholism. The early alcoholic will typically have a *greater tolerance* for alcohol, drinking more than his friends, yet showing the effects less. Thus, he may be among the last to leave the party, and he may be the person who drives others home because he is least affected by alcohol.

Another early symptom is a *growing preoccupation* with alcohol. The early alcoholic rarely will be caught with a refrigerator or liquor cabinet empty of alcohol, and he will probably include wine or beer on his shopping list before the eggs, bread, and pickles. Still, he does not necessarily drink every night, and when he does drink, he can usually control his intake so that he rarely gets drunk. He believes he is in complete control of his drinking, and when he does drink too much, he insists that he was just "in the mood" to get drunk.

In short, the early alcoholic does not appear to suffer in any way from drinking. He usually feels happy and carefree when he drinks. He may have frustrations, but they do not preoccupy him, and anxiety or tensions do not appear to drive him to drink. He is, in most cases, a psychologically and emotionally stable person. His childhood was normal, his family life comfortable; he is a patient father, a loving spouse, and a responsible employee.

If someone were to tell him that he was drinking too much, his reaction would be one of complete surprise. He is, after all, handling his liquor as well as or better than most of his friends; he rarely gets drunk, usually drinks at home with his wife or friends, and does not drink at lunch, in the morning, or even every day. On the surface, he seems to be a normal person who happens to enjoy alcohol and thus seeks the pleasure of its company more and more often. He sees no reason to be ashamed or evasive about his drinking and may even brag about his drinking prowess. He can "take it or leave it," he insists, and it seems clear to him and others that although he likes to drink, he certainly does not need to drink.

His family and friends do not see anything unusual in his drinking because he does not deviate drastically from their patterns of drinking. He may influence them to drink more, but they believe he simply likes to have a good time. The early alcoholic may be able to hold his liquor a little better than others, but that causes no alarm. He may look forward to drinking occasions, but that does not raise eyebrows either. His ability to drink large amounts of alcohol without falling down drunk may, in fact, inspire affectionate pats on the back and a reputation as the life of the party.

If someone who knew the disease well and understood its earliest symptoms were closely watching the early alcoholic's behavior, he would probably suspect the gradual increase in tolerance, the growing preoccupation with alcohol, and the ability to function normally with large amounts of alcohol in his body as probable early symptoms of alcoholism. Most professions, however, would hesitate to label this behavior "alcoholic drinking" because it just does not resemble the more blatant and obvious changes which occur later in the disease and which are most often associated with alcoholism.

The Middle Stages

Over a period of several years, Jack began to drink more often and a little faster than his friends. Instead of waiting until 5 p.m., he began to drink at lunch, or he sometimes left work early and had a few at the local bar. At parties he was the first to finish his drink, and he would quickly gulp down another. He rarely said "no" to an offer of a drink.

When his wife criticized him for drinking too much, he learned ways to disguise his intake. The bar became a regular stopover after work, and he kept a flask in his briefcase "just for emergencies." He also started drinking martinis because they had more impact than a regular drink.

He knew he was drinking too much, but he quickly dismissed the idea that he might be an alcoholic. After all, an alcoholic was someone who didn't care what he looked like, didn't care if he disgraced his family and friends—in fact, an alcoholic usually didn't have any family or friends! Jack knew he wasn't the type of person who could become an alcoholic. His upbringing was normal and happy, his wife and children loved him, and his friends were respected members of the community. Nothing traumatic or unusual had ever happened to him.

As the cells of the central nervous system gradually become addicted to alcohol, the alcoholic experiences specific changes in his drinking behavior. He may begin *sneaking drinks*, which is one way of hiding his growing dependence on alcohol. On the way home from work, the businessman alcoholic may stop at a bar and quickly down one or two quick drinks; the housewife may start drinking at 4 p.m. before her husband gets home. At a party, the alcoholic might go into the kitchen on the pretext of helping the cook, and, not incidentally, stiffen up his drink while there.

The middle-stage alcoholic will often loosen himself up before the party begins. This is called *predrinking*

drinking, and the goal is not just to get in the mood for a party but to help disguise his need to drink a lot of alcohol.

The way he drinks is also changing. The middle-stage alcoholic tends to *gulp the first drinks,* polishing off the first round and ready for the next before anyone else has finished. Once started drinking, he wants to continue—one or two drinks no longer satisfy him—and if others are showing signs of slowing down, he may order another round and attempt to liven up the conversation, hoping to prolong the drinking occasion. This behavior signifies the beginning of *loss of control.* The alcoholic may still be able to control when and where he begins drinking, but he cannot reliably count on being able to stop drinking once he has begun. With one or two drinks, the physical chain reaction begins which feels to the alcoholic and appears to others like a psychological demand for more alcohol. This inability to stop drinking once started does not occur every time he drinks, but it will gradually increase in frequency as the disease progresses.

As his ability to control his drinking gradually disintegrates, the alcoholic is placed in an extremely awkward position. He needs to drink because of the growing addiction, but he must also try to avoid getting drunk in order to escape both the severe withdrawal symptoms and the censure of his family and friends. It becomes extremely important to the alcoholic to prove to himself and others that he can still take alcohol or leave it alone. And so he develops his own unique *strategies of control.*

Alcoholics who discover that they regularly lose control with their first drink may go on the wagon for prolonged periods of time. Others may switch to beer or wine, drink only on weekends, only at taverns, or only after 5 p.m. Many middle-stage alcoholics can successfully control or appear to control their drinking throughout a period of probation set by a judge, employer, or spouse threatening separation or divorce. These temporary control strategies are often misinterpreted as evidence that the person is not addicted to alcohol and could control his drinking if he would only put his mind to it. Occasional "slips" are concealed or rationalized by the alcoholic and forgiven by the concerned nonalcoholic.

Thus, in the middle stage of alcoholism, the people who could exert pressure on the alcoholic to get help are instead blinded to the progression of the disease by the alcoholic's ability to control his drinking temporarily. Of course, most alcoholics will make a superhuman effort to control their drinking if a return to drinking out of control means jail, mandatory treatment, divorce, or loss of a job. In addition to keeping his marriage, career, and social status intact, however, the alcoholic's most important priority is protecting his continued freedom to drink, and he will cooperate with anyone who can make this possible.

Questions about his drinking cause the alcoholic concern and distress, and if anyone implies that he should stop drinking, his defenses slam shut around him. The middle-stage alcoholic will go to great lengths to avoid discussing his personal and drinking problems. If his wife or children ask him why he drinks so much or plead with him to cut down, he will avoid an answer by changing the subject or he may defend himself by blaming his drinking on someone or something else. If his doctor happens to question him about his drinking, he may answer, "Oh, I drink moderately, just like my friends." If pressed, he often becomes more evasive or defensive.

When his drinking repeatedly begins to interfere with his responsibilities or otherwise is annoying to others, the all-important question is raised: "Why does he do it?" Most people look for the psychological motive or reason, believing that alcoholics drink too much because of stress, anxiety, insecurity, or profound unhappiness. "If you loved me, you wouldn't do this to me," the spouse complains. "Don't you care about your children (or your job or your reputation)?" The alcoholic, feeling guilty and ashamed, asks himself these same questions and agonizes over his inability to control himself. Knowing nothing of his addiction, he must come up with reasons for his excessive drinking and destructive behavior. And so he learns to explain and rationalize his drinking episodes. "I was tired and depressed, and the drinks just happened to hit me hard"; "You've been nagging me all day, and I did the only possible thing I could do—drink to drown you out!" "We always get sloshed on Paul's birthday—you know that"; "They didn't serve dinner until 10 p.m., how in the hell was I supposed to stay sober?"

Society mistakenly believes that alcoholic drinking is a response to stressful problems, and the alcoholic from the beginning shares this belief. Later on, this confusion of the consequences of drinking with the causes becomes the fortress of rationalization from which the alcoholic defends his drinking. To himself he says, "My job is frustrating, my boss unfair, my spouse nags and puts me down, my children are spoiled and disobedient, I'm frustrated, bored, depressed, trapped in a lousy job and marriage."

By rationalizing his drinking problems and pinning the blame on others, the alcoholic is able to defend his integrity and self-respect and, of course, his right to drink. The drinking, he sincerely believes, is merely a response to far more serious life problems. He has become so totally wrapped up in these acceptable reasons for his drinking behavior that he fails to notice that they have become mere excuses. He loses all ability to judge his own behavior accurately, and in his ignorance of his underlying physical disease, he knows only that he must protect his freedom to drink.

At this point, he may *change drinking patterns* in the belief that the cause of his problems is the type of alcohol he drinks, where he drinks, or whom he drinks with. He may change brands or switch from Scotch to gin or bourbon to beer. He may stop seeing his nonalcoholic friends, convinced that their long faces and heart-to-heart talks are only making him drink more. He may try to drink only at home for a while in an attempt to get away from the "bad influences" at the tavern.

Changing jobs or moving to another town (known as *geographic cures* in Alcoholics Anonymous) represents another attempt to cope with growing problems. The alcoholic may decide that most of his troubles are related to his job ("It's demeaning," he complains bitterly; or "They expect too damn much of me"). He may blame the town he lives in ("It's too small; everyone is always poking their nose into other people's personal business"). And so he moves to another town, gets another job, or arranges a new work assignment, preferably traveling much of the time so he is free to drink as he wants.

The middle-stage alcoholic begins to experience frequent *mood swings* or *personality changes* when drinking. The quiet man may become obnoxious, the gentle man belligerent; the family man may begin to flirt with strangers; the swinging bachelor may become morose and disinterested in sex. As he continues to drink, he will begin to *lose his self-respect* and sense of personal integrity. He cannot find many reasons to like himself. He makes his family miserable by continuing to drink, constantly complaining, and blaming them for his unhappiness. His remaining friends are fast losing patience; they look at him with pity and disgust. When he wakes up after a drunk, he is overcome with *remorse* and *guilt*. His efforts to control his drinking have clearly failed once again; his wife eyes him with reproach, his children with anger and bewilderment. "Why am I doing this to them?" he asks himself. He cannot understand his own behavior, and he is frightened by the changes in his personality. "I'm just no damn good," he thinks, an opinion which only becomes more entrenched as he continues to drink.

Frightened and disgusted with himself, the alcoholic

gradually turns inward, away from people. He spends more and *more time alone,* no longer able to cope with his family's anguished questions or his friends' reproaches. He is overwhelmed with *self-pity,* which intensifies as his isolation grows. Everyone is picking on him, he believes, and he knows somehow that he is not completely at fault. On the other hand, he knows he should stop drinking, but he cannot. And so he drinks, risking everything else in his life for alcohol. To everyone else, his behavior seems self-destructive and suicidal; but for the alcoholic, drinking is self-preservation. He knows what it feels like to wake up with the shakes, and he knows the magic of alcohol in relieving them. He is trapped—more aware of the short-term torment of not drinking than of the long-term consequences of continuing to drink.

The middle-stage alcoholic's *emotions are strung tight.* He is usually tense and anxious unless he is drinking. One slighting remark or questioning glance, and he is immediately irritated. An unmade bed, a telephone call during the cocktail hour, a dirty bathtub, no more catsup, an unpaid bill, a driver honking his horn—any one event is enough to set him off. He explodes, screaming at the kids, cursing his wife, humiliating his secretary; then he stomps off. Later he feels guilty and ashamed. These emotional outbursts occur most often when the alcoholic is in withdrawal, and they only confirm to him his need for a drink. As soon as he takes a drink, he calms down.

The alcoholic's interaction with others becomes increasingly tense and strained. At first, his career, his marriage, and his personality flaws are blamed, and excuses are dredged up to rationalize his behavior. "It's probably my fault," the spouse worries. "I should be more patient with him." "He'll get over it," friends whisper. "It's just a phase he's going through."

But when it becomes obvious that the alcoholic's drinking is not just a phase, his family and friends become more outspoken in their concern. Because the middle-stage alcoholic's problems seem mainly psychological, the family may suggest that he see a psychotherapist or marriage counselor. His personal physician is just as likely to suggest psychiatric help because the signs of physical deterioration or damage appear to be secondary to the emotional problems and he may be unaware of the physiological basis of the disease. If the alcoholic is referred to a psychiatrist, his guilt and self-loathing are likely to deepen. The search for psychological causes of his drinking will only strengthen his feeling that he is to blame somehow. Not only may psychiatric treatment fail to help; it can actually be harmful since the search for psychological causes only reinforces the alcoholic's rationalizations and diverts attention from the physiological causes of the disease. Psychiatric exploration may go on for years, while the alcoholic continues to drink, and the physical disease goes on unchecked.

The family attempts to cope with the alcoholic's behavior in various ways. They may withdraw from all social occasions, embarrassed and ashamed for their alcoholic, or they may leave the house whenever possible, letting the alcoholic "stew in his own juice." Neither approach has any long-term effect, for the alcoholic continues to drink, and his psychological and behavioral problems worsen.

If the alcoholic does manage to go on the wagon or cut down, the family is encouraged and hopeful. Eventually, however, the hope turns to despair when the alcoholic returns to his old drinking patterns. All the efforts to talk, to scream, or to love him until he realizes he has to stop are of no avail; the more drastic measures of pouring full bottles of alcohol down the drain, booting the alcoholic out of the house, or calling the police also fail miserably. The drinking goes on, and in time it gets worse. Soon enough, any attempt by the alcoholic to change his ways is greeted with a tight-lipped nod, a silent and doubtful "We'll see." The family's existence is one of despair, a hanging-on filled with moments of fear and trepidation. "What will happen when I get home? Will he be drunk, passed out, or mean and sober? Will he be dead this time?'"

After countless attempts to make the alcoholic stop drinking, the family may believe they have no options, no encouragement, and no hope. Still, they may stick by the alcoholic, sensing that he is, at bottom, the sensitive and loving person they knew before, and knowing that he would not willingly hurt them—knowing, too, that something has taken over his mind and body. What it is, they do not know; they only pray that it can be cured or fixed before it is too late.

The middle-stage alcoholic has probably been having *blackouts* from time to time. Blackouts are a very distinctive feature of alcoholism, and one symptom that clearly distinguishes alcoholics from nonalcoholics. The events which occur during an alcoholic blackout are not forgotten; they are simply not stored or are imperfectly stored in the brain. There is nothing there to be recalled later.

During a blackout, the alcoholic may be functioning normally and aware of everything that is happening around him. He continues to talk, walk, eat, drive a car, conduct a business deal, or make love to his wife. Yet on sobering up, he has no memory trace of what occurred during a certain time period—it could be a minute, an hour, or even several days. In the early stages of the disease, blackouts are relatively infrequent, but as the disease progresses, they occur more often and last for longer periods of time.

Jack attended a series of weekend meetings held in a city 90 miles from his home. The last meeting ended in midafternoon, and Jack retired to the bar with several friends. It was happy hour, and the bartender announced a special on martinis: six ounces of gin for just $2.00. Jack drank four specials and then decided to order dinner before he drove home. With dinner, he drank a bottle of wine. It was late when he started driving, but he remembered watching the moon rise over the low hills. The next thing he knew and could later recall, he was travelling 110 mph and was 25 miles past his exit. He had driven 100 miles in a blackout.

It is not difficult to imagine how frightening blackouts can be. The alcoholic may wake up in the morning with no recall of the events of the previous evening. He gets out of bed, afraid to inspect his clothes—did he get sick? Then the question occurs to him: "How did I get home?" He looks out the window, fearful that the car will be missing. He does not remember driving home. The car is there, and he has another, even more frightening thought: "Did I hit something or someone?" He runs outside and looks at the front end. He searches the seats for clues to help him piece the lost time back together. Humiliating thoughts race through his mind: "Did I disgrace myself? Will my friends talk to me? How can I find out what happened when I am too embarrassed to admit that I don't remember?"

Blackouts can be so frightening that they make the alcoholic question his sanity. For the first time, he may realize that he is in deep trouble with alcohol. Despite his increasing problems, however, the middle-stage alcoholic rarely considers giving up drinking; he may believe a psychiatrist can help him sort out his "underlying psychological problems," but he cannot believe that drinking is responsible for those problems. It just does not make sense, because drinking makes him feel good, not bad. In fact, alcohol is the only thing he can count on to pull him through a tense day or a frustrating encounter. As a result, the alcoholic begins to *protect his supply,* always making certain that a bottle is hidden in the car, the house, or his desk at work—just in case he needs it.

Of course he needs it more, and more often. The withdrawal symptoms are becoming so severe that he drinks frequently and is in extremely bad shape when he stops drinking. Whether he admits it or not, the alcoholic needs alcohol to function, and he is ingenious in discovering places to hide it. The toilet tank and glove compartment are classic hiding places; more innovative caches include the steam compartment in an iron or the windshield washer compartment in a car. W. C. Fields allegedly kept a hidden supply of alcohol in his walking cane.

Soon enough the alcoholic is in *trouble at work*. Mondays are frequently missed because of weekend binges; lunches may last for two or three hours; colleagues who are tired of covering up and assuming the alcoholic's work load complain; rumors of bottles in his desk and whiskey on his breath filter through the office. The employer may shut his eyes, hoping the problem will go away by itself, but at some point, he will be forced to do something about his alcoholic employee. He may fire him based on the accumulated evidence; or he may give him the choice between treatment or being fired. This last option may finally make the alcoholic realize how serious his problem is. Alcoholic drinking takes a lot of money. The alcoholic's job feeds his family, pays the bills, gives him an identity, supports what is left of his self-respect, and holds together his fragile life style. To lose his job would be a financial and emotional disaster. No matter how sick he is, that fact will usually register—if only for the reason that, without a job, he will no longer be able to afford alcohol.

Toward the end of the middle stage of alcoholism, the alcoholic *neglects eating* because his inflamed digestive system rejects food. He keeps going instead on the easy energy of alcohol, which also alleviates the symptoms of gas, bloating, nausea, and heartburn. He may also experience a *decrease in sexual performance*. As Shakespeare wrote, drink "provokes the desire, but it takes away the performance" (*Macbeth*, Act II, scene iii).

Numerous *doctors' visits*, referrals to psychiatrists, and *hospitalizations* may take place toward the end of the middle stage of the disease. *Psychiatric treatment* or counseling may continue for many years, but as long as the drinking continues, the alcoholic's marital, work, and personal problems can only get worse. As this happens, the alcoholic is frequently given *prescriptions* for sedatives, tranquilizers, antidepressants, or sleeping pills to relieve his mental and physical misery. These substitute drugs are harmful to the alcoholic even if taken as prescribed. As with alcohol itself, the superficial benefits only mask deeper penalties. At best, the alcoholic will switch and become addicted to the prescription drug and continue to deteriorate. But because of cross-tolerance, he will typically increase the dosage in an attempt to get the desired effect.* Since the drugs lack calories and are a poor substitute for alcohol, the alcoholic is very likely to switch back to alcohol or to drink while taking the drugs, a practice that complicates and aggravates his symptoms and is often fatal.

The Deteriorative Stage

Jack knew that something was seriously wrong. He couldn't sleep, and he was constantly nervous and tense. Any little annoyance or disruption of his routine made him irritable.

He finally agreed to see a doctor, who prescribed tranquilizers for his tension, told

---

*See chapter 10 for a discussion of cross-tolerance.

him he was working too hard, and advised him to slow down. But the irritability and tension persisted, and in fact, Jack began to feel worse. He stopped taking the pills because they weren't helping anymore. Alcohol worked better and faster. At least when he was drinking, he felt in control again.

He was drinking every day now, and most of the day. His wife threatened to leave him if he didn't quit drinking or get help. Finally, she filed for divorce. Everything fell apart after that. He lost his job and most of his friends. He had recurring thoughts of suicide, but they only intensified his drinking. His wife got the house, and he spent his last months in a cheap rooming house. One evening after drinking a quart of whiskey, Jack passed out with a lighted cigarette in his hand. He died in the fire.

Morning drinks become habit in the final stages of alcoholism. At first the alcoholic starts to drink in the morning to silence the withdrawal symptoms. He cannot hold a pencil without dropping it. The coffee cup shakes in his hand until he spills half the contents on his lap. His heart feels as if it would hammer right out of his chest. He is queasy, nauseated, paranoid, and terrified. He must drink if he is to stop the shakes, and he drinks in the morning before he allows himself to see anyone; he drinks again in the car on the way to work; and he nips at the bottle in his desk until it is time to go to lunch where he throws down a few more.

Soon enough the alcoholic is not able to keep up this charade, for he too often *overdrinks his tolerance* and gets drunk. He can no longer choose when or where he drinks; he must drink all the time, wherever he happens to be. The ever-impending withdrawal symptoms have become so excruciating that the alcoholic is compelled to drink just to delay them. He has no choice but to drink, because alcohol is the only cure for his physical and mental torment. Loss of control is complete. The late-stage alcoholic escapes the overwhelming need to drink only when unconscious, but the blessed relief of unconsciousness is only temporary. As the alcohol is eliminated from his body, the withdrawal symptoms build up, and the alcoholic awakens to an overpowering need for a drink.

Soon there is no distinction between morning, noon, and evening; only the time of drinking and the time of unconsciousness or exhausting nausea exist. The cycle continues around the clock. *Prolonged binges* are now the rule, and the alcoholic drinks continuously for days or weeks until he becomes so sick that he must stop. *Hospitalizations, suicide attempts,* and *arrests* for driving while intoxicated or public drunkenness are frequent consequences of these binges.

By this time, the late-stage alcoholic has probably lost his job and is *financially dependent* on his family or the welfare system. His habit is expensive, but he has no money to pay for it; and so he does anything he must to get alcohol. He panhandles, borrows from his friends, steals from his wife's pocketbook, smashes his children's piggy banks. If the money situation gets too desperate, he may resort to drinking anything that contains alcohol, including vanilla extract, canned heat, shaving lotion, cough syrup, or rubbing alcohol. This practice may also land him in the emergency room or mental ward.

He begins to *drink alone or with inferiors* in seedy taverns or in the hallways of dilapidated rooming houses. He avoids previous haunts because he is terrified of meeting someone who might recognize him. He cannot even wind his watch or unzip his fly, and his shame locks him inside the four walls of his room, alone with his only remaining friend, alcohol. He is incapable of thinking rationally both when he is drinking and when he is in withdrawal. His attention span is short, he cannot follow a conversation, and he has difficulty speaking clearly.

Paranoia and *vague fears* begin to haunt the late-stage alcoholic's waking hours. The slightest noise—telephones ringing, the doorbell, a person's voice, a child's scream, a faucet dripping—makes him jump and stare wild-eyed. He is terrified of strangers and may be convinced that people are talking about him or planning to lock him up. His fears are magnified during withdrawal, and the only cure for them is more alcohol. Even alcohol, however, has lost much of its magic. Now it doesn't really make him feel good; it only eases the shakes and the pain. After just a few drinks, he is either drunk or violently ill.

Eventually the reality of what the alcoholic's life has become can no longer be ignored. The rationalizations, denials, and excuses crumble, and the alcoholic is left with the spectacle of his wasted and broken life. He may seek permanent and immediate escape from this crushing knowledge through *suicide;* he may fear both death and life without alcohol and so continue to drink until death puts an end to his misery; he may experience *vague religious or spiritual desires,* hoping for a miracle to pull him out of the mess of his life and return his sanity and self-respect; or he may begin to look for help. Tragically, help usually consists of a brief drying out period, after which the alcoholic simply returns to his old life style. He may be given pills or told to report to an out-patient counseling program. With this minimum level of help and support, the late-stage alcoholic has only a slim chance of starting a recovery from his disease.

The alcoholic's addiction is now obvious to even the most casual observer. He is the classic picture of the Skid Road bum.* All the family's efforts appear to have ended in failure, and failure breeds fear, frustration, and resentment. The alcoholic's spouse and children may lash back at him; screaming, hysterical battles may rock the household and destroy any remaining hope of an end to the long and bitter tragedy. The family may suddenly stop fighting and simply give up, convinced that they can only provide the alcoholic with a warm place to sleep and food to eat. Or, having lost all hope, they may pack up and leave him to his misery.

Whatever course the family takes, they are usually as emotionally sick as the alcoholic. The wife or husband may feel responsible; he or she also feels worthless, incompetent, useless, and unloved, and suffers crippling guilt and self-pity. The alcoholic's children are also battle scarred. All the solid foundaticns of love, security, and predictability have been knocked out from underneath them, and they are frightened and torn apart with doubts and fears: "Will he die? Does he hate me? Is it my fault? Why can't I do something?"

The late-stage alcoholic is usually isolated from his friends and relatives. Social contacts have disintegrated. Neighbors lower their eyes. Relatives may be so paralyzed by anger or grief that they, too, stop trying. The alcoholic "problem" is ignored, put out of mind, locked away where it cannot hurt so much. The late-stage alcoholic is not totally alone, however, for he is in frequent contact with the caretakers of our society—the policemen, social workers, doctors, emergency room personnel, and public health nurses. These are the people who will either refer him for effective help or finally pull the sheet over his head.

Help must come fast for the late-stage alcoholic, but it must be the right kind of help. With effective intervention and treatment, even the most advanced,

---

*As A.A. members say, Skid Road is not a geographic location, but a condition between the ears.

deathly ill alcoholic may recover. The human organism has extraordinary abilities to restore or compensate for damaged tissues. The surviving cells can regenerate, poisons can be flushed out, and the body can begin the slow process of healing itself. Most alcoholics now sober were once considered "hopeless" by the people close to them.

8

Getting the Alcoholic Into Treatment

I doubt if any alcoholic ever wakes up, looks out the window, and says, "This would be a nice day to go for rehabilitation. I think I'll call the doctor." He may not see the gun, but some type of pressure—outside forces or his health—motivates him.

Thomas Fleming, M.D.

Without help, most alcoholics cannot permanently quit drinking. A combination of factors works to imprison the alcoholic within his addiction. In the early, adaptive stage, before social and psychological problems develop, neither the alcoholic nor those around him see any reason why he should stop drinking. As problems do begin to develop, the heavy drinking is generally seen as merely a symptom, and the alcoholic may be advised to get help with his "underlying problems." Later, when the heavy drinking itself is clearly contributing to his problems, he and others are more likely to conclude that he should cut down on his drinking, not that he should quit altogether.

Typically, only when the more blatant symptoms of alcoholism develop, does anyone suggest that the alcoholic ought to stop drinking completely. By this time, the alcoholic's mental processes are firmly under the influence of the addiction, and his need to drink pushes aside all rational concerns about the harmful consequences of continuing to drink. He may come to realize that he should stop drinking, and under pressure, he may even go "on the wagon" for a while. But without a new perspective on the problem and a sustaining force powerful enough to override the addiction, all such periods of abstinence are temporary.*

More often, the alcoholic will reject any idea that he should stop drinking. Dimly he may realize that his problems are connected with drinking, but the addiction blinds him to the fact that alcohol is causing those problems. Alcohol is his first aid and his medicine. It is the effective remedy for the psychological and physical pain that ails him, immediately relieving his anguish and tension, stopping his hands from shaking and his stomach from heaving, allowing him to think more clearly and act more normally, and particularly in the later stages of the disease, providing the only moments when he is released from suffering. When he stops drinking, the real trouble begins. The tension, frustrations, tremors, irritability, and nausea finally become so unbearable that he has to drink because alcohol is the quickest way to relieve the pain.

The alcoholic needs help, and he needs it as early in his disease as possible. The widely accepted belief that alcoholics have to "hit bottom" before they can be helped has been completely discredited in recent years. Waiting for the alcoholic to realize he needs treatment is simply a mistake, for left to his own devices, he is likely to become less willing to seek treatment, not more willing. If treatment is delayed until the alcoholic is so ravaged by his disease that his liver and brain are

---

*Comprehensive treatment and A.A. are the most powerful weapons against addiction, but alcoholics have been known to achieve permanent sobriety following a religious conversion or even more rarely after a particularly frightening incident such as a blackout or a near fatal accident.

permanently damaged, his wife has given up on him, his employer has fired him, and he is living on welfare, it may have been delayed too long.

The alcoholic who can stand on his feet, who still holds a job, and whose marriage is intact may insist that he does not have a problem and stubbornly refuse to get help. He may lie, steal, and cheat to protect his right to drink. But his deceptions and refusals are no indication that treatment will fail. No matter how fiercely the alcoholic fights those who want to help him stop drinking, he can be helped more often than not. Well over half of the alcoholics now being treated successfully were forced into treatment against their wills; they did not want to stop drinking, but certain crises in their lives backed them into a corner and forced them to seek help. For one alcoholic, the motivating force may have been his wife's threat to pack up and leave if he did not get help; another alcoholic may have finally agreed to enter treatment after getting drunk and smashing his car into a bridge abutment. Early- and middle-stage alcoholics have been pushed into treatment by spouses planning divorce, employers threatening loss of jobs, judges offering the choice of treatment or jail, landlords threatening eviction, and doctors warning of fatal consequences if drinking continues.

Guidelines for Helping

Rather than waiting for such a crisis to occur, strategies have been developed in recent years to deliberately create a crisis and to use it to coerce the alcoholic into treatment. Anyone who hopes to help an alcoholic should follow five basic guidelines.

Learn About the Disease

Understand the nature of the chemical alcohol, how alcohol affects the alcoholic and the nonalcoholic in different ways, and why the alcoholic continues to drink when drinking is obviously harming him. Learn about the early-, middle-, and late-stage symptoms of the disease and how these symptoms change as the alcoholic continues to drink. Learn about the underlying physiological changes, including adaptation, tolerance, physical dependence, and the withdrawal syndrome, all of which have a profound effect on the alcoholic's behavior. Finally, learn why the alcoholic needs to drink, why he becomes irritable, frustrated, and depressed when he is not drinking, and why his sincere promises to stop drinking are washed away like writing on sand.

Avoid Moral Judgment

The alcoholic is a sick person, not a bad person. He needs compassion and understanding, not anger and indifference. Moral judgment and condescending attitudes only make the alcoholic defensive and hostile and push him even further away from treatment.

Develop An Emotional Detachment

The person trying to help must understand that the alcoholic is both physically and psychologically sick and that his behavior is governed by his addiction. When drinking or between drunks, the alcoholic acts in bizarre and unpredictable ways. At one moment, he may be consumed with self-pity and sincere promises to change his ways; moments later, he may angrily deny that he has a drinking problem and become belligerent or indignant when anyone suggests that he does. Remember that the alcoholic believes what he has been taught—that alcoholism is a symptom of underlying psychological and social problems. He interprets the facts as evidence that his drinking is caused by events outside his control.

If the alcoholic's family or friends become emotionally embroiled in these excuses and denials or believe that they are somehow responsible for causing the alcoholic's unhappiness, the real problem—the physical addiction—will get sidetracked, and the psychological symptoms will be mistaken as the source of all the trouble. The helper must remember that his first and most important priority is to get the alcoholic into treatment and off alcohol. Only after his body has a chance to recover from its long, poisonous alcohol bath can there be a return to psychological and emotional stability.

Pick a Specific Treatment Program

Not all treatment programs are the same, and some treatment programs are simply not effective in helping alcoholics recover. Those who are trying to help the alcoholic into treatment should understand the limitations of various treatment programs. Out-patient programs, for example, offer counseling services but have no in-patient medical facilities; most general hospitals provide brief in-patient detoxification but offer no real alcoholism treatment as such. A.A. is not really a treatment program, as it provides no detoxification facilities, medical support, or professional counseling services—but as a program for helping the alcoholic to maintain sobriety after treatment, A.A. is the best there is.

The early-, middle-, and late-stage alcoholic will have the best chance of recovering if he is treated in a comprehensive, disciplined program that includes the following:

• In-patient medical detoxification;
• A 4-week minimum of in-patient care;
• Educational programs which stress the physical basis of the disease and its role in causing psychological and social symptoms;
• Intensive nutritional therapy and education;
• Strong emphasis on A.A for long-term sobriety;

- Thorough follow-up care;
- Involvement of the family in treatment and follow-up care.*

If possible, the family, employer, or friend should select an in-patient program that comes as close to these criteria as possible. Not every city has such a program, however, and if the only ready options are out-patient programs or A.A., they should by all means be tried. Just one warning, however: If the alcoholic returns to drinking, the family and friends should not give up, saying, "We tried treatment, and it didn't work." They should instead try to find a program that gives the alcoholic a better chance of recovery; and if that treatment fails, they should try again and again. While relapses are discouraging, they are not the end of the road. In fact, most alcoholics now sober have had at least one relapse on the way to lasting sobriety.

Finally, the alcoholic must not be allowed to pick his own treatment program because he will invariably select a program that provides the least interference with his drinking. An out-patient program that requires only an hour a day with a counselor, or a weekly A.A. meeting, would be more to his liking than a 4-week minimum in-patient program which would completely cut off his access to alcohol. His primary reason for rejecting in-patient treatment will be denied and masked by the argument that he can't afford the program or that he can't take the necessary time off from work.

Get Help

A careful "confrontation strategy" must be worked out in advance. When Betty Ford's family sat her down and outlined why they thought she had a drinking problem, their words were carefully rehearsed. Under

---

*The features of an effective comprehensive treatment program are more fully discussed in chapter 9.

the guidance of a physician and nurse from a successful treatment program, the family members had prepared what they were going to say. Mrs. Ford's excuses, denials, anger, and tears were all expected, and the family knew how to use the confrontation to force her to a realization of her addiction.

Anyone who hopes to help an alcoholic into treatment will need help himself. The first step might be to look in the yellow pages under "Alcoholism Agencies" or "Alcoholism Treatment Programs." Talk to counselors and treatment staff, ask specific questions, and demand specific answers. "What do I do if he ignores me, becomes angry, or refuses to talk?" "How do I convince him that he needs treatment?" An excellent description of confrontation strategies is contained in Vernon Johnson's book, *I'll Quit Tomorrow.*[1] The National Council on Alcoholism also publishes guidelines for confronting the alcoholic, as does the CompCare Corporation, one of the better private sources of information on alcoholism.[2]

Attend some A.A. and Al-Anon meetings. A.A. has open meetings which anyone can attend; just call the A.A. number listed in the phone book and ask for specific times and meeting places. Al-Anon is an organization patterned after A.A. but specifically designed for the concerned nonalcoholic. Both A.A. and Al-Anon offer the family and friends of alcoholics the solace of knowing that they are not alone and that others have been through similar or worse ordeals.

Who Can Help?

The Family

Of all the people who can help the alcoholic into treatment and support his recovery after treatment, the alcoholic's spouse and children may be the most effective. The family has first-hand experience with the alcoholic, they know how serious the drinking problem is and how far it has progressed, and they often have the emotional power to force the alcoholic into treatment.

The family's deep emotional involvement with the alcoholic can also be a burden, however. The family may be so desolated by the alcoholic's behavior that they are paralyzed with grief and guilt and unable to help. They may be so filled with shame that they hide the problem and refuse to discuss it with anyone. Or they may be so familiar with the alcoholic's suffering when he stops drinking that they are reluctant to ask him to stop.

In order to help the alcoholic, the family must learn as much as they can about this disease and understand that they are not responsible for the alcoholic's behavior. Nothing they have said or done has caused the alcoholic to act the way he does. The disease itself is responsible for the alcoholic's behavior and personality changes. By learning about the disease, the family can keep an emotional distance from the problems and understand why he acts the way he does and what they can do to help him.

The family must also understand that the alcoholic has to stop drinking or he will continually get worse. Waiting until he realizes the extent of his problem is waiting too long, for the family itself may be destroyed by their involvement and, without his family, the alcoholic is less apt to get help.

The family can let the alcoholic's physician know the extent of the problem and enlist his help in getting the alcoholic into treatment. The spouse can explain the facts of the disease to the children so that they understand their alcoholic parent's behavior and what must be done to make him well again. The family can also talk to friends and relatives, outline the problems at home, and make sure that they too understand the seriousness of the alcoholic's continued drinking.

A major problem at this point may be one of misguided loyalty. The family may feel disloyal when they reveal confidences or plot confrontations behind the alcoholic's back, and the alcoholic, of course, will cry "traitor" if he gets wind of his family's intrigues. But the family cannot rely on the alcoholic to help himself. They demonstrate their true loyalty when they do everything in their power to help him get well.

When devising a strategy for confronting the alcoholic about his disease, the family should seek enlightened professional counsel. Specialized treatment staff, A.A. members, physicians, clergymen, and community alcoholism counselors may all be of help in choosing the best available treatment program and planning the confrontation.

Finally, having enlisted the help of the alcoholic's friends, relatives, and physician, armed with knowledge about the disease and how it can best be treated, and backed by professional advice and counsel, the family can squarely confront the drinking problem. Refusing to accept the alcoholic's denials and evasions, the family members can calmly and firmly tell him that he has a disease, he needs help, and help is available. The alcoholic must know that the family is not bluffing, and the family should therefore be prepared to follow through on any threats made.

This road is not an easy one. The alcoholic may deny his problem, throw tantrums, or weep with self-pity. There may be ugly quarrels and moments when hope and optimism are just too painful to hold on to. Friends and relatives who do not understand the disease may believe the family is overreacting. Encounters with unenlightened physicians, psychiatrists, and other professionals who insist that the alcoholic is psychologically or emotionally disturbed rather than suffering from a physiological addiction may be frustrating and confusing.

Once the alcoholic's spouse and children know the facts of the disease, however, they can do something about it; and doing something for the alcoholic is, however difficult, less painful than continuing to be involved in his slow death. Covering up, ignoring, or denying the disease is a sure way to prolong the agony. If the alcoholic keeps drinking, the disease cannot get better—it can only get worse.

The Employer

The alcoholic's employer can wield enormous influence over his decision to enter treatment. It is the employer who can pose the critical choice: Enter treatment or lose your job. As former Congressman Wilbur Mills once said, "An alcoholic may be insane, but he's not crazy. He'll go to a facility any time rather than lose his job. He has to have money to finance his habit."[3]

In order to exercise his power over the alcoholic, the employer must understand the disease, gather his evidence carefully, and then, preferably with the family's knowledge and consent, clearly explain the facts to the alcoholic. These confrontations are most effective when they are conducted by several people the alcoholic knows and respects and when the evidence is presented clearly and without moral condescension or judgment. For example, the employer might say:

> "John, last Friday a group of your fellow employees picked you up off the floor of the bar next door and deposited you in a taxi cab. You cursed and attacked the driver who immediately opened the door and kicked you out. You went back into the bar where you called your assistant a whore and accused her of trying to steal your job, punched an innocent bystander in the jaw and then passed out on the table. Three weeks ago, the janitor found an empty whiskey bottle under your desk. Another employee tells me you insulted a customer at lunch last week and told him to take his 'filthy business' elsewhere; he called me today and canceled his account. Last month

you were sick 5 days; last year you took 40 sick days. I have reports here from your supervisors, complaints from the people who work with you, customer complaints, and a list of your sick days and accident reports—and they all add up to a serious problem. We believe you have a chronic and progressive disease, and we want you to get well. You are a valued and respected employee. But we cannot allow this to continue any longer. For your sake and for the sake of this company, we must offer you a choice: either go for treatment, or you are fired. I'm afraid that is all there is to it."

Such a factual presentation squarely backs the alcoholic into a corner. He is no longer able to pretend that his life is normal or that his drinking does not interfere with his work. The hard evidence is there, and his boss is not kidding.

The employer's emotional distance from the alcoholic is another powerful weapon. The alcoholic's family will frequently accept the blame for his drinking and suffer from confused feelings of guilt, inadequacy, and shame. Many families are unable to leave the alcoholic or force him out of the house because they fear that will destroy him rather than help him. The employer, on the other hand, has a business relationship with the alcoholic, and he is usually able to maintain a professional detachment. Unlike the family members, the employer is specifically concerned with the economics of the situation, and he can verify his observations with facts from the personnel record or written reports from other employees. He can document hours of work missed, sick days, complaints, and supervisor comments and then clearly and unemotionally present these facts to the alcoholic.

Employer confrontations are successful also because the employer is dealing with an alcoholic who is still able to come to work and at least keep up a semblance of normal behavior. If the alcoholic is still working, he is probably in the early or middle stages of his disease. He still has some pride and sense of personal integrity, his physical and mental health are not too impaired, and his job is usually extremely important to him. All these factors help fuel the alcoholic's motivation to get and stay sober.

Unfortunately, confrontations at work are only possible for those alcoholics who do work. Women alcoholics, for example, have traditionally been more difficult to diagnose and treat because their performance is less likely to be judged by anyone outside the family who has some basis for bringing pressure. This is changing as more women enter the work force, but for all alcoholics who work alone or at home, the family's participation in forcing treatment becomes even more imperative.

The Physician

The family physician can be pivotal in alcoholism treatment, helping the alcoholic to realize the serious medical consequences of drinking, providing information and referral to an effective treatment program, and supporting the alcoholic's sobriety after the specialized treatment. The strictly medical aspects of their role are quickly learned. Effective patient management, however, requires much more than mere relief of acute medical symptoms. In order to be really helpful, the physician must acquire special knowledge of the disease, its causes and progressive symptoms, and learn how to guide the patient into treatment. Because few medical schools include any significant education or training in alcoholism, the average physician needs to do some self-education. Reading in the alcoholism literature and attending some A.A. meetings are good places to start.* Most physicians

---

*See the Suggested Reading List, p. 191.

soon learn, however, that they can make the most effective use of their time and talent by working closely with an alcoholism specialist, preferably one who is himself a recovered alcoholic with a good quality of sobriety and who is active in both a professional role and in A.A. Through this association, the physician can soon familiarize himself with the various treatment programs, costs, admission procedures, and staff liaison so that he can advise the alcoholic about specialized treatment.

Once educated about the disease, the physician is in a position to be particularly helpful. He can:

- Diagnose the disease in its early stages, recognizing the psychological symptoms of depression, irritability, moodiness, and anxiety for what they are—evidence of the underlying physiological disease of alcoholism;
- Go beyond half-hearted warnings such as "You should cut down on your drinking" and instead outline exactly what will happen to the alcoholic if he continues to drink;
- Recommend specific treatment options and explain the advantages and disadvantages of each;
- Maintain regular contact with the alcoholic, following up on the referral to make sure that the alcoholic gets into treatment once he is diagnosed;
- Involve the family in helping to motivate the alcoholic into treatment and then help the family to deal with any problems that may arise after treatment;
- Encourage the alcoholic's attendance at A.A. meetings;
- Warn the alcoholic about the risks of taking drugs of any kind—particularly sedatives, tranquilizers, and antidepressants, which are addictive and interfere with alcoholism recovery;
- Warn the alcoholic about taking any medication or foods that contain alcohol.*

*See Appendix A for a list of such medications.

The alcoholic must almost inevitably go through a series of crises before he is able to recognize the seriousness of his disease. The physician can speed this process along by helping the alcoholic face the realities of his drinking behavior and, at the same time, by letting him know that help is available. Most importantly, the physician can refuse to give up on the alcoholic. Alcoholics can often miss appointments, stubbornly deny drinking problems, and continue to drink despite serious warnings. The physician must understand that the alcoholic's behavior is governed by his addiction and that he is incapable of acting in a normal, responsible fashion whether he is drinking or between drunks.

Policemen, Judges, and Attorneys

Policemen are in constant contact with alcoholics, picking them up for drunk driving, car accidents, vagrancy, street fights, theft, assault, disorderly conduct, and public drunkenness. The police officer is not a diagnostician or a social worker, but given appropriate training, he can learn that alcoholics are not primarily criminals or mentally disturbed individuals but victims of an addiction they are helpless to control. The policeman's response can then be one of compassionate discipline rather than disgust. He will understand that the alcoholic's problems cannot be solved either by punishment or by a hot meal and a place to sleep. Instead, the alcoholic may need medical care to help him through withdrawal or for other complications associated with alcoholism. In both subtle and obvious ways, the police officer can influence the alcoholic to see himself as a sick person who needs special help.

Judges know well that people with legal troubles often also have drinking problems. A person with a history of DWI ("driving while intoxicated" or "driving while under the influence") arrests, car accidents, divorce, and financial problems is very likely an alcoholic in need of specialized help. If the judge suspects alcoholism, he can require the offender to be diagnosed and evaluated by a competent alcoholism specialist. If the diagnosis is alcoholism, the judge can then use his full powers to get the alcoholic into the recommended treatment program.

Whenever possible, judges should require an effective in-patient program. But if out-patient treatment is the choice, the alcoholic should be put on notice that if he returns to drinking he will be immediately remanded to in-patient treatment. A minimal two-year probation period should be established, and the alcoholic's sobriety should be monitored closely during probation. The most effective treatment programs are those requiring A.A. attendance during probation.

Enlightened attorneys are also in a position to identify the alcoholic client and motivate him toward effective treatment. The alert attorney knows that legal problems and alcohol problems go hand-in-hand. He can ask detailed, personal questions of his client, and since the client ususally expects these questions, he answers them freely. He listens to the attorney's advice because he needs to have his problems solved, he is dependent on the attorney to help him, and he knows that if he refuses to heed the advice, severe legal penalties may await him.

Again, the attorney is not a trained diagnostician or alcoholism counselor, but he can learn the symptoms of alcoholism, and he can refer his clients to an alcoholism specialist for diagnosis and recommendation. The attorney can then use every weapon in his arsenal, including his powers of argument, patience, and perseverance, his familiarity with the painful consequences of repeat offenses, and his knowledge of available treatment programs to direct the alcoholic into effective treatment.

Alcoholics Anonymous

A.A. is the best program in existence for helping alcoholics to stay sober, but it is not a particularly effective vehicle for getting the alcoholic sober in the first place. A.A. is not a treatment program because it has no detoxification facilities or staff, no 24-hour medical care, no professional counseling services, and no authority to ensure patient compliance with a treatment regimen. An alcoholic who attempts to get sober through A.A. must detoxify himself, a difficult and painful process that only a few alcoholics endure without resorting to alcohol for relief from withdrawal. Bill Wilson, the cofounder of A.A., lamented the fact that, in his estimation, only 1 alcoholic in 18 was able to start his sobriety in A.A.

Many A.A. members do not trust formal treatment programs, however, and therefore do not advise the alcoholics who are struggling to get sober on their own to seek in-patient treatment. Historically, there are understandable reasons for this distrust. A.A. members are all too aware of the condescension and judgmental attitudes about alcoholism which pervade conventional health agencies. They have been drugged with tranquilizers and sedatives, have spent expensive and fruitless years in psychotherapy, and have endured indifferent and even hostile professional attitudes toward them and their disease. Most A.A. members believe that only an alcoholic can help another alcoholic, which is the basis of the belief that only alcoholics can lead alcoholics to sobriety. These beliefs are founded in experience, for not until they come into A.A. do many alcoholics find others who really understand their problems and can help them to accept the disease and stop drinking. The long-standing antagonism to alcoholism treatment programs appears to be lessening, however, as programs emerge which are based on an understanding of the addiction, staffed by recovered alcoholics, and emphasizing A.A. attendance for staying sober. But some degree of distrust lingers on.

Another tenet of A.A. philosophy which works against early treatment is the idea of "hitting bottom," generally expressed as the belief that alcoholics can be helped only when they realize the hopelessness of their condition and are willing to accept help. This belief is also changing, but A.A. is generally a self-help organization, and many members still cling to the idea that the alcoholic must first come to grips with his problem and then get himself into treatment.

Finally, A.A. is of limited help in getting the alcoholic into treatment because it lacks potent leverage. Unlike the spouse, the employer, the physician, or the attorney, A.A. does not have the power or influence necessary to force the alcoholic into treatment by threatening an even less attractive alternative.

A.A. members do, however, have the wisdom of experience. They have suffered through the disease, and they can tell the alcoholic what to expect if he continues to drink. As A.A. members take a more aggressive stance by encouraging others to confront the alcoholic and help him into treatment before he hits bottom, countless numbers of alcoholics are being spared the suffering and humiliation of the later stages of the disease.

Friends

Friends often do more to hurt than help the alcoholic. They are frequently guided by the misconception that alcoholism is an emotional weakness and are therefore unwilling to attach the label "alcoholic" to someone they love and respect. They are also accustomed to defending their friend against criticism because "that is what a friend should do." By failing to recognize that the alcoholic has a serious and potentially fatal illness, a friend may actually be placing a subtle pressure on the alcoholic to keep drinking in order to prove that he is, indeed, a "normal" drinker.

Even if the friend wants to help, he often feels frustrated and helpless. He may make tentative advances, only to have the alcoholic become hostile and defensive.

"What can I do?" he may ask. "It is not my place to tell him to stop drinking!"

Yet the alcoholic's friends can help. Armed with correct information, a friend can help the alcoholic realize his problem and confront it. The friend must also learn, however, how to approach the alcoholic. If he attacks, the alcoholic will defend, and no good will come of the encounter; if he approaches with understanding and compassion, the chances that the alcoholic will listen and act are much greater.

Friends can also talk to the alcoholic's family and encourage them to seek help. They can refuse to be manipulated by the alcoholic's rationalizations and denials and make clear to the alcoholic that he has a problem and needs help. The alcoholic may simply ignore the friend's advice, or he may be so furious with his friend for threatening his continued freedom to drink that the friendship may not survive. But the risk is worth it. A friend who refuses to support the alcoholic's continued drinking is expressing his concern for the alcoholic's life. This concern may make a profound difference.

Acquaintances and Associates

The person motivating the alcoholic to seek help need not be an intimate friend, family member, or someone with formal or tacit authority over the alcoholic such as a judge or physician. Many alcoholics have been guided into treatment by casual acquaintances or associates such as teachers, taxi drivers, hospital orderlies, or landlords.

The critical determinant of whether an individual can help is not who he is but how well he understands the disease. His attitude toward the alcoholic will also affect the alcoholic's willingness to listen and respond to advice. A sympathetic and knowledgeable taxi driver can be more help to a drinking alcoholic than an uninformed physician who refers the alcoholic to a psychiatrist or gives him tranquilizers and sends him home. A landlord who serves his tenant with a court order offering the choice of eviction or treatment does more to force recognition of the problem than the woman who buys her husband liquor every day because she knows he feels better when he is drinking.

The point is that anyone can help push the alcoholic toward treatment. The basic tools needed are a comprehensive knowledge of the disease, an understanding that the alcoholic is physically and emotionally sick and that his behavior is governed by his addiction, a recognition of the fact that he is unable to help himself, an ability to be emotionally detached, and a refusal to participate in fear, guilt, shame, anger, or pity.

9

A Guide To Treatment

It's a long road to a good sobriety. But I can wait. I can put one foot in front of the other. Life has meaning if not perfection. I'll be with my family tonight and find joy in being with them. I'll get up tomorrow and go to work—without cold sweat, headache, and misery in just the thought of another day of exertion with another hangover. I don't have life all worked out—I never will, or there would be no challenge to it. But working on the mystery of it has its own rare rewards. There's a chance for happiness now. I didn't have that before.

A recovered alcoholic

Historical Perspective

In 1804 Thomas Trotter, an Edinburgh physician, wrote a paper stating his belief that habitual drunkenness was a disease:

> In medical language, I consider drunkenness, strictly speaking, to be a disease, produced by a remote cause, and giving birth to actions and movements in the living body that disorder the functions of health.[1]

Trotter's essay provoked an explosive controversy that continues to this day. In one sentence, he challenged the moral code of a society, threatened a basic tenet of the Christian church, and questioned the medical profession's traditional lack of involvement with the drunkard. Ever since Trotter, society has been deeply divided over the question: Is alcoholism primarily a physiological disease, or is it, after all, a symptom of character inadequacy and emotional weakness? This is still the root source of conflict and confusion in the alcoholism field today.

The church's vehement opposition to Trotter's essay was based on several points. By elevating "depravity" to the status of "disease" and insisting that the victim was not responsible for his actions, Trotter threatened society's moral code, over which the church stood guardian. Throughout history, the habitual drunkard was considered a sinful and pitiful creature who, preferring vice to virtue, was responsible for his many troubles. This was part of the moral code which proclaimed: Drunkenness is bad; moderation is good. Drunkards are to be pitied and despised; abstainers are virtuous and admirable.

If excessive drinking is a disease, as Trotter proclaimed, the drinker cannot be held responsible for his own actions and is thus protected from moral condemnation and judgment. By shifting the blame from the alcoholic's character to a "remote cause" outside the alcoholic's control, Trotter's new theory confused the lines between "good" (that is, will power, self-control, and moderation) and "evil" (that is, weakness of character, gluttony, and intemperance).

The medical profession was equally upset by Trotter's essay, which suggested that the treatment of this "disease" was mainly their responsibility. The physician's involvement with the drunkard had been limited to treating the physical complications accompanying excessive drinking, performing autopsies, and signing death certificates. The average physician viewed alcoholics with the same mixture of fear and disgust expressed by the rest of society, and most had no desire to spend their time ministering to men and women who presumably lacked motivation and ambition, consorted with unsavory characters, and carelessly threw their lives away in pursuit of debauchery.

Without the moral approval of the church or the professional cooperation of the physician, the fledgling "disease concept" did not catch on. In fact, the first attempts to treat alcoholism as something other than a mental or social aberration encountered fierce and effective opposition. Almost a quarter century after Trotter's essay appeared, Eli Todd, medical superintendent of the Hartford Retreat for the Insane, suggested that it might be better to give "inebriates" a separate retreat rather than lump them with the insane and mentally incompetent. His indignant colleagues forced him to abandon the idea. A similar suggestion by the Connecticut State Medical Society two years later was also hastily scrapped for lack of support.

Not until 1841, when the Washington Home first opened in Boston, was an "institution for inebriates" able to withstand public disapproval and keep its doors open. The next sixty years witnessed an age of enlightenment in the study and treatment of inebriates; by 1900 over fifty public and private facilities had opened for the sole purpose of treating inebriates. In 1870, the American Association for the Cure of Inebriates (soon renamed the Association for the Study of Inebriety) was founded by a group of physicians and superintendents of inebriate asylums. In 1876 the Association launched the Quarterly Journal of Inebriety, which, until it ceased publication in 1914, stimulated research and discussion by publishing hundreds of articles on alcohol-related issues.

Yet despite these significant advances, most people continued to view drunkards as moral degenerates rather than the innocent and unwilling victims of a disease. The church insisted that the chronic inebriate was responsible for his unhappy state and needed the church's moral guidance to be reformed. The belief that alcoholism was a disease failed to ignite the interest of most physicians, and their acceptance of this revolutionary concept was half-hearted, at best.

Almost one hundred years after Trotter's essay first generated heated controversy, the moral and religious attitudes toward drunkards and drunkenness were, if anything, even more intense and intolerant. By the end of the nineteenth century, the burgeoning Temperance movement had organized a crusade against alcohol at the national level, launching attacks from the pulpit with Bibles in hand and hymns of salvation firing passions. The Volstead Act, establishing national Prohibition in 1919, effectively eclipsed further study of alcoholism as a disease. Although Prohibition did reduce total alcohol consumption in the country, it had no apparent effect on alcoholism and thus missed its mark. As typically happens with misguided attempts to legislate morality, Prohibition not only failed to curb the original problem; it added a host of others. Bootlegging, hijacking, and syndicated crime became so widespread that the whole experiment had to be abandoned.

Shortly after the repeal of Prohibition in 1933, an event occurred which reinstated alcoholism as a subject worthy of scientific interest and, at the same time, ushered in the present age of compromise and confusion. In 1935 the fellowship of Alcoholics Anonymous (A.A.) was begun by two men who had been given up as "hopeless" drunkards by their physicians. Both men were able to stay sober, and they went on to help thousands of other alcoholics recover in a program that relied on simple spiritual principles and the compassion and understanding of fellow sufferers to achieve total abstinence from alcohol. A.A. demonstrated for the first time that alcoholics in significant numbers could recover and return to productive, useful lives. Most importantly, it proved that alcoholics, when they stayed sober, were decent, normal human beings and not hopeless degenerates.

The significance of these insights was undermined, however, for A.A. had also embraced the moral attitudes of the day: while asserting that alcoholism is a disease, the program fixed the blame for contracting the disease squarely on the victim. In *Alcoholics Anonymous*, the A.A. "Bible," and in *Twelve Steps and Twelve Traditions*, A.A.'s cofounder Bill Wilson refers repeatedly to "glaring personality defects" and "character flaws" that caused excessive drinking and thus alcoholism:

> We reluctantly come to grips with those serious character flaws that made problem drinkers of us in the first place, flaws which must be dealt with to prevent a retreat into alcoholism once again.[2]

Thus, from its inception, A.A., like the rest of society, has mistaken the psychological consequences of alcoholism for its causes, and the moral approach of the program followed logically. The Christian formula of sin, repentance, and redemption can be clearly seen in A.A.'s Twelve Steps, especially Steps 4 through 7:

Step 4: Made a searching and fearless moral inventory of ourselves.

Step 5: Admitted to God, to ourselves, and to another human being, the exact nature of our wrongs.

Step 6: Were entirely ready to have God remove all these defects of character.

Step 7: Humbly asked Him to remove our shortcomings.[3]

Despite its moralistic foundation, however, A.A. worked as no other approach to alcoholism had before, and as a long-term sobriety maintenance program, there still is not even a distant rival. Thus A.A. stands as a colossal paradox. The fellowship has undoubtedly been the most powerful force in getting society to accept alcoholism as a treatable disease. Yet at the same time, it has become a powerful obstacle to accepting the otherwise overwhelming evidence that biological factors, not psychological or emotional factors, usher in the disease.

Nevertheless, A.A. has helped tens of thousands of alcoholics to get and stay sober. Inspired by A.A.'s early success, several major developments followed; like A.A., they moved the disease concept forward but also retained the belief that the onset of the disease is caused by defects of character. In 1940, the Quarterly Journal of Studies on Alcohol was established within the Laboratory of Applied Physiology at Yale University. Now titled the Journal of Studies on Alcohol and published by the Rutgers Center of Alcohol Studies at Rutgers University, this publication renewed scientific interest in the physiological and biological aspects of alcoholism, and reestablished alcoholism as a "field" worthy of scientific research. Once again, however, this influential effort was undermined by the age-old assumption that the cause of the disease was to be found in some mysterious character flaw or personality defect.

Having encouraged the development of the Quarterly Journal at Yale, Marty Mann, one of the first women members of A.A., also founded the voluntary lay organization which was later to become the National Council on Alcoholism (NCA). Along with A.A., NCA has helped to spread the idea that alcoholism is a treatable disease, while also maintaining the belief that psychological problems are the primary predisposing factors.

The impact of these developments was enormous, and the church and medical profession were finally forced to modify their positions. One hundred forty-two

141

years after Trotter's essay, the Presbyterian Church became the first religious organization to acknowledge formally alcoholism's status as a disease. Note, however, the allowance for moral censure in the qualifying phrase of the proposition accepted at the Church's 158th Assembly in 1946:

> *Once drinking has passed a certain point,* alcoholism is a disease; that is, the drinking cannot be stopped by a mere resolution on the part of the drinker. [Italics added]

The medical profession shuffled its feet for another ten years until the American Medical Association (AMA) finally "voted" alcoholism a disease in 1956. Yet even here the disease concept was seriously compromised, for the main body of the medical profession continued to view alcoholism as a self-inflicted symptom of an underlying psychological inadequacy and relegated treatment of the disease to its psychiatric branch, where it still languishes.

From this brief history, it should be clear why alcoholism continues to be the arena of such intense conflict and emotional turmoil. Students of the disease have tried to have it both ways, proclaiming loudly that alcoholism is a treatable disease and at the same time continuing to affix the blame and stigma for contracting the disease on the character of the unwitting victim. Both scientists and treatment professionals striving to advance the disease concept of alcoholism defeat their own aims by continuing to believe, or condoning the belief, that alcoholism is caused by heavy drinking, which in turn is caused by defects in the drinker's psychological, social, and cultural fabric. This is the belief that keeps alive all the age-old myths and misconceptions and the stigma, shame, and contempt for the alcoholic that continue to cloud the field of alcoholism.

Failure to recognize and dispose of this cancerous root results in a host of conflicts. Since the parties to the conflict are not dealing with the real problem, they end up fighting and arguing about superficial or irrelevant issues. Thus, even as scientific information accumulates explaining the hereditary physiological causes of alcoholism, professional attitudes remain stagnant and mired in myth and misconception. In Wallgren and Barry's encyclopedic *Actions of Alcohol*, the authors comment:

> It is difficult to develop understanding of a subject which arouses strong emotions and deep prejudices. The large amount of information available about alcohol is mingled with a great deal of misinformation, and much of the literature is distorted by emotion and burdened with an evaluative purpose, either to attack or to defend the social use of the beverage. Most facts are used to support the evaluative conclusion that "alcohol is evil" or "alcohol is innocuous." *Accordingly, most of the literature on alcohol has little scientific value.*[4] [Italics added]

On the whole, the major professions and the established hospitals and health agencies in the community are mired in this confusion and have therefore been unable to provide truly effective help for alcoholics. Outside the establishment, however, a grass-roots movement inspired by A.A. has given rise to a proliferation of specialized private and public treatment programs for alcoholics, many of which are effective. Today, there are thousands of these programs, and they come in a bewildering variety of philosophies and practices—inpatient and out-patient, hospital-based and nonhospital, long-term and short-term, medical and nonmedical, intensive and less so, and more to the point, effective and ineffective.

Virtually all the effective programs have in common the understanding that alcoholism is a disease that can be arrested but not cured and that the cornerstone of full recovery must be continuous total abstinence from alcohol and substitute drugs. Nearly all these programs also usher their patients into A.A. for long-term sobriety maintenance after treatment. But, unfortunately, even these programs, which are relatively successful, base their treatment philosophies and strategies on the A.A. belief that the alcoholic disease begins with a character flaw or other psychological inadequacy, and this belief is the major shortcoming among otherwise effective treatment programs everywhere.

By treating the psychological problems as primary rather than the physical disease and addiction, programs which could otherwise help 80+ percent of their patients make lasting, high quality recoveries instead can only claim recovery rates half that high and a relatively poorer quality of sobriety for their patients. These programs typically underestimate or miss completely the long-term effects of toxicity, malnutrition, hypoglycemia, and even the withdrawal syndrome in causing or aggravating the alcoholic's psychological problems. Instead, the recurring psychological problems are mistaken as evidence that the alcoholic is, at bottom, an inadequate, depressed, anxious, and self-destructive personality. This view of the alcoholic's character and personality, as stressed throughout this book, reinforces the sick alcoholic's belief that he is responsible for his disease, increases his guilt and shame, intensifies his anxiety and resentments, and stiffens his defensiveness against both the diagnosis of alcoholism and the proposed treatment. These aggravated symptoms then loom up as the major problems to be

144

"diagnosed" and treated rather than as the symptoms of an underlying physical disease.

A high proportion of treatment programs, especially outpatient programs, rely on "cold turkey" withdrawal, that is, withdrawal without benefit of medical care. Of the treatment programs that do provide medical management of withdrawal, only a small minority provide intensive nutritional analysis and therapy. This may be another legacy of A.A., in which most of those who have achieved any significant period of sobriety started out "cold turkey."

Regardless of the treatment method, the majority of recovered alcoholics have not had adequate diagnostic evaluations or treatment for their primary disease and its complications, for hypoglycemia, or for other nutritional complications. The most noticeable lingering symptoms of this neglect are chronic psychological problems. It is fair to conclude that the quality of their sobriety is not high. In fact, it has been seriously compromised by their treatment.

This relatively low quality of sobriety has been the only general norm available to researchers. It has therefore become the standard for evaluating recovered alcoholics and for comparing various treatment alternatives. To be more specific, if treatment programs are not based on a real understanding of alcoholism as a physical disease, and if the medical and nutritional needs of patients are neglected, then it does not really matter whether treatment occurs in an in-patient or an out-patient setting. If all an in-patient program has to offer is "cold turkey" withdrawal and alcoholic orientation, then the staff will probably find it hard to justify holding the patient for longer than two or three weeks. And since the success rate (30 to 40 percent) and quality of sobriety (seriously flawed) of such a program can also be achieved in a purely out-patient setting, then many would argue, with some justification, that the out-patient form should be favored for economic reasons.

So long as arguments about the type and duration of treatment are based on a lack of understanding of alcoholism as a physical disease and on low standards of success, treatment programs are not likely to improve. Unfortunately, both public policies and decisions by insurance companies concerning the funding of alcoholism treatment are presently being based on norms from these inadequate treatment programs.

Because of the widespread limitations on the quality of treatment available, a word of advice is in order for the reader who is an alcoholic in need of treatment. First, rule out any program that does not at least have total abstinence as a treatment goal and also any program that prescribes substitute drugs beyond the acute withdrawal period. With these exceptions, go ahead and try the treatment available. Don't jeopardize your recovery by criticizing the program while you are still in it. Concentrate instead on the things offered that will help you to stay sober. A.A., for example, is in nearly every community, and attending their meetings will be most helpful.

The important point is that sobriety has to have first priority, for without it no other significant life improvements are possible. If you do stay sober, you will have plenty of time in the future to find ways to improve on nutrition and otherwise improve the quality of life in sobriety. You are not alone, and you will find many other recovered alcoholics seeking the same objective.

Clearly, however, it is time to establish a higher standard of treatment based on a new awareness of the physiological basis of the disease as presented in this book. A program that treats the disease of alcoholism as a primary, physiological disorder will view the patient's psychological complaints and disturbances as symptoms

146

of the disease he is living with and of the desperate
state he is in. The staff will know that the disease has
created a grotesque caricature of the underlying person.
The alcoholic's anger, fear, depression, immaturity, and
defensiveness will be treated for what they are: the
outpourings of a sick brain. By consistently treating the
patient's negative behavior as a symptom of his disease,
the staff will let the alcoholic know that his condition is
thoroughly understood. This approach will be enormously
reassuring to the sick alcoholic as he comes to realize
that not he but the illness is being blamed for his
behavior and that his treatment is aimed at relieving his
suffering and treating the underlying disease. The entire treatment sequence and the attitude of the staff
toward the patients will be shaped by this understanding.

Such a treatment program has existed since 1970.
The Alcenas Hospital program was founded expressly as
a demonstration model of the understanding of alcoholism presented in this book.[5] Except for the nutritional
components,* the Alcenas program may outwardly sound
like many others—a private hospital exclusively for
alcoholics (both male and female), a 24-hour medical
staff to help with detoxification and continuing medical
care, a 4-week minimum of in-patient treatment, lectures,
films, tapes, group and individual counseling, group
and individual family therapy, 12 weekly follow-up group
counseling sessions, and A.A. participation during and
after treatment. What makes the program unique,
however, is the nutritional element and the fact that the
content of the lectures and all other communications
with the patients are expressions of the revolutionary
understanding of alcoholism presented in this book.

The optimum treatment sequence as dictated by the

---

*The nutritional program includes nutritional analysis (laboratory workup, hair
analysis for the mineral profile, five-hour glucose tolerance test, skilled staff
evaluation), and intensive nutritional therapy.

disease itself and as tried and proven in over eleven years of practical application at Alcenas Hospital is described in the remainder of this chapter.

A Model Treatment Program

Phase I: Getting Started

The first treatment priorities are to gain control of the addiction and to find out exactly what is wrong with the patient. The best way to achieve these objectives is to get the alcoholic into a hospital or other in-patient treatment center with a medical staff and modern medical facilities. The patient simply has a better chance of recovery if he is placed in a controlled medical setting where his drinking can be stopped with certainty, medication can be used to control the withdrawal symptoms, laboratory workups can be conducted to assess complications and nutritional needs, diet and nutritional supplements can be fully controlled, and a competent medical staff can be on hand 24 hours a day to handle any emergencies and to monitor progress.

An alcoholic detoxified in a nonmedical setting suffers unnecessarily and may be in grave physical danger. An untrained, nonmedical staff may inaccurately diagnose the alcoholic's complaints, and neglect underlying physical problems such as pneumonia or infections. Without adequate laboratory procedures, the alcoholic's physical health cannot be effectively assessed and monitored. In-patient medical care, on the other hand, provides priceless insurance against medical complications and severe withdrawal symptoms and gives the alcoholic the comfort and security he needs during the sometimes traumatic first days of treatment.

Effective treatment includes a thorough medical examination, bed rest, fluids as indicated, medication to prevent the more serious withdrawal reactions, and a balanced diet with vitamin and mineral supplements as individually indicated. Injectable supplements should be available and used in the first few days of treatment or until the patient is able to absorb and utilize oral supplements. With this care, the withdrawal syndrome presents no serious problems for the majority of alcoholics.

Some alcoholics will be prone to grand mal convulsions, hallucinations, extreme mental confusion, or dangerous fluctuations in blood pressure, temperature and pulse rate during withdrawal. These symptoms typically occur in more advanced alcoholics, or in patients with major medical complications such as liver disease, hemorrhage, pneumonia, heart disease, and gastrointestinal disturbances. An alcoholic who has been drinking a fifth of whiskey daily for several weeks is also a likely candidate for these major withdrawal symptoms. With intensive medical care, however, even the most severe withdrawl symptoms can be prevented or minimized.

Because histories taken at the time of admission are notoriously unreliable, it is sometimes difficult to determine which patients are at risk for the more serious withdrawal reactions. Therefore, all the sick patients should be given a controlling level of tranquilizing medication as a preventive safety measure. The drug dosage should then be decreased each day and typically discontinued after a few days of treatment. After the acute withdrawal period, no mind-altering drugs should be used. However, other medications necessary for the control of heart disease, diabetes, or epilepsy may be used as required.

After a few days in detoxification, the crisis is over for most patients. The withdrawal symptoms fade, and the alcoholic feels better and can begin to think more clearly. Some treatment programs, notably state or county detoxification centers, release the alcoholic at this point, when he is "dry" and the worst of the withdrawal symptoms appear to be over. Unfortunately, the addiction is still strongly in control during this period, and too often the first thing the alcoholic does after leaving the treatment center is find a drink. Thus, the alcoholic who is hospitalized for three or four days, detoxified, given a bottle of vitamins and/or depressant drugs, and then released has not been adequately treated. His hands will shake, his cells will cry out for alcohol, he will continue to be confused, depressed, and fearful. He will almost invariably drink again as soon as he leaves the protection of the treatment center, because he does not yet have the ability to choose not to drink.

Treatment must be more than an interlude between binges. It must do more than get the alcoholic dry and back on his feet. It must go on to get him started in a new life of sobriety.

Phase II: Into A New Life Style

After a few days of good food, nutritional supplements, rest, medical attention, and abstinence from alcohol, most patients experience a noticeable transformation. Clouded eyes clear, hands stop shaking, posture straightens, thinking becomes more rational, and depression, insomnia, and paranoia begin to fade. At this point, most patients are ready to begin the second phase of treatment: learning about their disease and what they must do to cope with it.

Some alcoholics—particularly, late-stage, severely malnourished alcoholics with medical complications such as cirrhosis or gastritis—may require a longer time in detox and may not be able to absorb new information as quickly or completely as the relatively healthier patients. The treatment program should recognize that every patient is different despite the fact that they all suffer from the same basic disease, and allow extra time for those patients who are having difficulty thinking clearly, concentrating, remembering, or relating to other people.

Educating the alcoholic about his illness would not be such an important or difficult part of treatment if everyone in society understood the disease and why certain people cannot drink "normally." But misunderstandings abound, and the alcoholic himself is always confused about his disease. He must be reeducated, told why he is an alcoholic, what he must do to get well, and how he can protect himself against internal and external pressures to drink when he leaves treatment. Information and education alone cannot keep an alcoholic sober, but they are essential to the patient's motivation and ability to learn the life style that will protect his sobriety. The three main elements of this protective system are understanding the nature of the disease; nutritional discipline; and A.A. participation.

Understanding The Nature Of The Disease. The alcoholic must fully and completely understand his disease—how it occurs, how it has affected his personality and behavior, why he is depressed when he stops drinking, why alcohol makes him feel better, why he experiences the urge to drink, why he cannot ever safely take a drink, why he will return to drinking if he is not protected—in short, all of these questions must be confronted and answered. Once he understands his disease, he will also understand what he must do to control it.

The alcoholic must also understand that he is not responsible for the things he said or did when he was drinking. The physical addiction controlled his behavior, and because he is powerless over the addiction, he cannot be held responsible for it. When the alcoholic looks back at his life as a drinking alcoholic, he should learn to say, "That's what alcohol did to me," not "That's what I did." Saying the words "I am an alcoholic" should convey the same moral overtones as the words, "I am allergic to pollen."

In counseling sessions, the alcoholic should be encouraged to confront his drinking life, but there should be no attempt to analyze his behavior or dig down and uproot past traumas, psychological problems,

151

or conscious or unconscious conflicts. Efforts to analyze the alcoholic's drinking behavior in these terms only heighten his guilt, shame, resentments, and frustrations. The purpose of counseling should instead be to build up his self-confidence and self-respect and to encourage normal interactions with other patients and the treatment staff. The emphasis should be on the present and the future, not the past, and the alcoholic should be taught to disown his past behavior as foreign to his true nature, as actions dictated by a sick and poisoned brain. He must come to believe that he could no more control his reaction to alcohol than an epileptic could control the activities in his brain causing seizures.

Once the alcoholic understands his disease and what it takes to stay sober, however, a moral obligation does enter the picture. *Now he knows:* If he follows the sobriety maintenance program, he will stay sober; if he willfully or carelessly deviates from the program, he will drink again and inflict the illness on himself and others. He has a clear choice now, and he should feel the moral imperative to make the right choice. If he relapses after undergoing truly effective treatment, he cannot be absolved of responsibility, as he was in the first instance. But if he is willing to start over with a more sincere effort to follow the program, he can be quickly forgiven and fully accepted into treatment once again.

Nutritional Discipline. Nutritional therapy is critical to successful treatment, and yet it is a neglected or slighted feature of almost every treatment program in the country. The alcoholic must receive vitamin and mineral supplements in order to repair the cellular damage caused by years of drinking. Given proteins, vitamins, and minerals in correct amounts and proportions, the cells will be able to generate new cells, repair injured cells, and strengthen their defenses against other diseases. Also important is a high protein, low carbohydrate diet, which will control the alcoholic's chronic low blood sugar and prevent the symptoms associated with this condition, including depression, irritability, anguish, shakiness, headaches, and mental confusion. If, after treatment, the alcoholic maintains a life-long dietary regime with appropriate vitamin and mineral supplements, his addiction will remain dormant, and he will not be threatened by the craving for alcohol that plagues so many alcoholics for months and years after their last drink.

Why, then, do so many treatment programs ignore or downplay the powers of good nutrition? Physicians, who receive little or no training in nutrition in medical school, are often wary of nutritional "cures" and extravagant claims about the powers of vitamins and minerals to restore physical and mental health. While their skepticism is sometimes warranted, there is no question that what we eat profoundly affects our emotions and other psychological processes. Furthermore, when a patient is chronically malnourished, as most alcoholics are, long-term nutritional therapy is obviously required to restore physical and mental health, and ignoring such patients' nutritional needs is simply inadequate treatment.

Hypoglycemia sparks even more controversy in the medical profession. A number of books published in the 1960s and 1970s made sweeping claims that hypoglycemia is a disease of epidemic proportions and the cause of disorders as varied as schizophrenia, suicide, drug addiction, divorce, crime, apathy, family disintegration, and moral decay.* Aware of the lack of documentation and research to support these claims and the swelling numbers of patients who diagnose themselves as hypoglycemic, many physicians have gone to the other extreme, claiming that hypoglycemia is actually a

---

*See the Suggested Reading List under "Nutrition" for several works taking a measured view of hypoglycemia and the role of nutrition.

rare condition and that most patients who believe they are hypoglycemic are actually suffering from purely psychological problems.

While the diagnosis of hypoglycemia may be mistakenly used by people to explain unrelated psychological and emotional problems, there is no question that the great majority of alcoholics suffer from chronic low blood sugar. When given the 5-hour glucose tolerance test, over 95 percent of both early- and late-stage alcoholics experience a spike in blood sugar level after intake of sugar and then a rapid plunge. If their erratic blood sugar level is not controlled, alcoholics suffer chronic symptoms of depression, irritability, anguish, fatigue, insomnia, headaches, and mental confusion. Worst of all, low blood sugar causes a craving for substances such as alcohol and sweets which can quickly raise the blood sugar and relieve the symptoms. Sober alcoholics, therefore, must learn to control their sugar intake in order to avoid mood fluctuations, anxiety, and depression, and recurring impulses to drink.

Some treatment programs do emphasize a high protein, low carbohydrate diet during treatment but assume that, once the alcoholic stops drinking and is off alcohol for several weeks or months, his nutritional problems are solved. The healing process can take several years, however, and if the alcoholic neglects his diet after months of sobriety, his body will have a difficult time completing the repair work. Because some of the damage—in the liver and elsewhere—is often permanent, continued supplementation will be needed to offset continued deficiences. Low blood sugar will also remain a chronic condition which will surface continually unless it is controlled through diet.

For all these reasons, nutrition should be emphasized from the start of treatment. Under medical supervision, the patient should be given a complete lab workup, a 5-hour glucose tolerance test to determine his sensitivity to sugar, and a hair analysis to help assess specific vitamin and mineral deficiencies. Coffee and refined carbohydrates including pastries, desserts, and candies should be strictly avoided because they cause abrupt changes in blood sugar levels and aggravate hypoglycemic symptoms.*

During treatment the alcoholic should be informed about his need for specific vitamin and mineral supplements, and taught how to plan his diet and how to read labels to determine the sugar content of various foods. The treatment program should emphasize the critical importance of continuing the hypoglycemic diet and supplements after discharge. The alcoholic must learn that this nutritional program is an intergral part of a life-long sobriety maintenance regime which will protect him against a craving for alcohol and the depression, irritability, and anxiety associated with hypoglycemia.

Alcoholics Anonymous Participation. A.A. is far and away the most effective program in the world for helping alcoholics to stay sober. In fact, helping alcoholics to stay sober is the primary purpose of A.A. Most recovering alcoholics, however, have the same reservations about A.A. that nonalcoholics have, envisioning A.A. members as a group of losers and scruffy fanatics speaking a mumbo-jumbo of love, spiritual renewal, and brotherhood. With this image in mind, most alcoholics shun the thought of A.A. meetings—because the fellowship frightens or repulses them or because they believe that they do not need it and can stay sober on their own. Left to their own devices, then, most alcoholics will not become involved in A.A.

The treatment program should therefore routinely do everything possible to increase the alcoholic's familiarity with A.A., requiring the patients to attend meetings while in treatment and encouraging them to discuss their reactions to A.A. Most alcoholics need to

---

*See Appendix C for a sample hypoglycemic diet.

attend twenty or thirty meetings before they feel at home in the fellowship and fully appreciate the need for it.

A.A.'s strengths are, of course, formidable. Most alcoholics need protection against the permanent threat of their addiction; A.A. offers shared experience, strength, and hope. Most alcoholics flinch from looking at their past; A.A. helps them to face their lives as alcoholics, accept their disease, and keep in touch with it so as not to lapse into wishful thinking that they can drink again. Most alcoholics have some difficulties getting started on a sober life; A.A. offers guidance, support, and discipline.

Yet for all its strengths, A.A. is not perfect, and the recovering alcoholic should be warned of A.A.'s shortcomings. First, A.A. is not a treatment program, and alcoholics who walk in off the street have a very rough time trying to stay sober. The alcoholic who is just starting a new life of sobriety should realize this fact and not be disheartened by those A.A. members who stop attending meetings and start drinking again.

The recovering alcoholic should also beware of the A.A. belief that character flaws or personality defects cause alcoholics to get into trouble with alcohol, a belief which simply has no basis in fact. The alcoholic should be assured throughout treatment that his personality did not cause his disease and that he is in no way responsible for it. This assurance will rid him of years of accumulated guilt and shame and help him to understand that abstinence is essential for the simple but very real reason that he is physically incapable of processing alcohol in a normal way. If he believes that his personality caused his disease, he may then believe that once his personality problems are fixed, he can return to normal drinking. Furthermore, a guilty and ashamed alcoholic may rebel against a program that aggravates these feelings and forfeit his sobriety in the process.

Patients should be taught never to base the 4th

step—"Made a searching and fearlesss moral inventory" —on a review of their past drinking behavior. Instead, the inventory should be based on their conduct *after* detoxification and enlightenment about their disease and the recovery process. A helpful way to take the inventory during the first weeks and months of sobriety is to answer the following question: "Now that I have a chance to start a full recovery, am I doing all in my power to comply with the program, to fulfill my moral obligation to stay sober, and to increase the quality of my sobriety?" As time goes by and the alcoholic gets a clearer, more complete picture of who and what he is in sobriety, he can add other guidelines and questions to this original one and update the inventory at intervals to ensure continuing personal growth and progress in sobriety.

Finally, the alcoholic should understand the grievous error in the A.A. belief that it is acceptable and even beneficial to drink coffee or tea and to eat foods high in sugar such as candies or ice cream when depressed, anxious, irritable, or feeling the need for a drink. This is dangerous first aid, for while caffeine and sweets have the immediate effect of elevating the alcoholic's low blood sugar, their use is followed soon after by a sharp drop in blood sugar, thus intensifying the hypoglycemic symptoms. Worst of all for the alcoholic, an unstable blood sugar level often leads to an impulse to drink if not an outright conscious craving for alcohol. It seems clear that hypoglycemia is a primary cause of the mood fluctuations and "white knuckle" sobriety so often seen around A.A. and also a major cause of "slips."

Phase III: Staying the Course

Over a period of years, alcoholism has a devastating effect on all aspects of the victim's life. Although only he has the primary disease, families become participants in the illness and often become as emotionally sick as the alcoholic member. They need to recover, too, if they are to adapt to the alcoholic's new sober life style. The alcoholic may be compulsive about his A.A. attendance, leading the family to believe that he cares more about A.A. friends than them. On the other hand, they will be alarmed if he stops attending A.A. meetings or gets off his nutritional program. How do they cope if he has spells of depression or irritability? They may even come to believe that it was easier to live with the alcoholic when he was drinking.

If the family members are to understand the problems that can arise during recovery and how they can help solve them rather than contribute to them, they must learn about the disease, the importance of diet and nutritional supplements, and the value of A.A. in helping the alcoholic to stay sober. At the same time, they must know and accept the fact that the alcoholic has the primary responsibility for his sobriety maintenance program. Whenever possible, the family should be involved in the treatment program and in follow-up sessions after treatment.

While sobriety requires adjustments and compromises from the family as well as the alcoholic, it need not be a time of constant depression, frustration, or fears that it may not last. The alcoholic must understand that doubts and fears are normal but that all problems can be solved without resorting to alcohol. Because he cannot turn to alcohol or drugs for relief of tension and frustration, he will have to learn how to deal with life's blows without giving in to resentments, self-pity, envy, or anger. Just trying to be normal is not good enough; he must reach for a higher level of maturity and self-knowledge than the nonalcoholic achieves, for he must cope with greater difficulties without resorting to chemical relief as they can and regularly do.

As sobriety continues, everything else will gradually improve. The alcoholic will soon learn that anything he could accomplish with alcohol he can do better, and enjoy more, without it. He will remember his drinking past for the hell it really was, and understand that there is no problem that drinking would not make worse. At first, as he watches others drink and enjoy themselves, he will feel deprived of something good. Later, he will feel gratefully rid of something bad. He will be able to say to himself, "Thank God I don't ever have to go through that again."

The Patient's Response to Treatment

The success of treatment is a function not only of what is done for the patient but also of what the patient does for himself in response to treatment. The patient's attitude and behavior toward his disease, his family, the treatment staff, and fellow alcoholics must undergo fundamental transformations if treatment is to be successful and sobriety secure. These transformations occur in three basic stages: submission, understanding, and commitment.

Submission

The first significant change required in the patient's attitude toward treatment is his willingness to submit to the illness and the treatment program. Submission does not require that the patient be enthusiastic or even motivated when he begins treatment. In fact, most alcoholics initially fight the diagnosis and the need for treatment and resent anyone who helped to put them there. If treatment is to progress and be successful, however, the patient must at least comply with the rules of the program and submit to the authority of the treatment staff.

When the alcoholic first starts treatment, he is, with rare exceptions, confused, frightened, and clearly in deteriorated mental and physical health. His brain is fogged by long-term exposure to large amounts of alcohol, and he cannot think or reason clearly. He may be hostile and defensive. Nevertheless, something has forced him into treatment—marital difficulties, car accident, hospitalization, court mandate, or suicide attempt— and he is probably very aware that he is desperately sick and needs help.

As he accepts the competent help provided, he begins to realize that he has come to the right place. He does not need to defend, because he is not being attacked. He is not being punished or made to feel ashamed of himself. His suffering is minimal, as the staff does everything possible to make him comfortable. With these newly ignited feelings of hope and health, the alcoholic can, at least, submit to the treatment program, and the process of recovery can begin.

Barbara, aged 50, a dance teacher and mother of two teenaged children, finally entered treatment when her husband threatened to leave her if she did not do so. He had threatened separation before, but Barbara realized he was deadly serious this time. During her last drinking binge, she had swallowed a handful of sleeping pills. She was drunk when she took them, and she still did not know whether she intended to kill herself or just get a good night's sleep. But her good or bad intentions did not affect her husband's decision to solve the problem in one way or another. He had had it, and he offered her the final choice: treatment or divorce.

On the drive to the treatment center, Barbara drank from a pint of whiskey, and on arrival she was feeling angry and belligerent. "Alcoholics," she sniffed, looking with distaste at the nurses, secretaries, and patients. "These people may be alcoholics, but I'm not one of them. What the hell am I doing here? I don't belong in this place!"

The image of a Skid Road alcoholic flashed in her mind, and she shuddered. She was not old and decrepit, her brain full of water, her eyes clouded, a stinking old bum. She was attractive, slender, wealthy, and middle-aged. "Why am I here?" she asked herself again.

She was escorted to the medical wing, where she glumly answered the nurse's questions and passively submitted to a physician's examination. She was then given a hospital gown and instructed to wear it until she was released from "detox."

Despite the gown and the outer trappings of a hospital, Barbara was surprised how liberal the rules were. After a day of laboratory tests, she was encouraged to walk around, go to meetings, read, and talk to the other patients. The afternoon of her second day, she walked into the patient lounge to have a cigarette. A man in the corner of the room watched her silently and, trying to be friendly, said "Welcome to the Club."

"Some club," she thought to herself, stuffing out her cigarette and marching out of the room.

She thought a lot about drinking that first week. She did not want to stop. She liked to drink, and sometimes it seemed that a drink was the only friend she had. Her children lived their own lives, her husband worked late, the dance classes were often frustrating, and the students were inept and clumsy. "Anyway," she reasoned, "alcohol makes me feel good. Maybe I was drinking too much and too often, but I can cut down. As soon as I get out of this place, I'll prove it to them all that I can drink like everyone else."

Yet despite her anger at being in treatment and her fear of living without alcohol, Barbara knew she had no choice. She was stuck here, for better or worse. Her husband was going to leave her if she didn't stop drinking, and he meant it this time. She did not believe that much could come from this treatment, but she was trapped and knew she had to give it a try.

Understanding

After several days of rest, good nutrition, and medical attention, the withdrawal symptoms subside in intensity, and the patient becomes accustomed to the treatment center and staff. He is sleeping better, able to think more clearly, and his hands have stopped shaking. The daily lectures begin to make some sense, counselors and staff are not such ogres after all, and other patients actually begin to look human.

Scattered pieces seem to come together. In the daily lectures, the emphasis is on the fact that alcoholism is a disease with certain identifiable symptoms. These symptoms are all familiar: the frustrations, unbearable tensions, vague fears, and problems at home and at work. As he relates the lectures and discussions to his own life, the disease begins to make some sense, and he begins to understand why he acted the way he did. He understands that he is not a self-destructive or suicidal personality; he simply cannot process alcohol in the same way the majority of people can.

As his understanding of the disease grows, the patient finally realizes how sick he was before he made it into treatment. He understands that his depression, anxiety, irritability, the fights with his wife, and the fears of insanity were all the results of a brain poisoned by alcohol. As he begins to feel better, he also understands how close he was to losing everything—his family, his job, his health, and his life.

At this point, the recovering alcoholic may feel an urgent need to completely reorder his life and try to fix everything that was destroyed when he was drinking. He wants to apologize to all the people he hurt in the past, and he feels a need to get right to work on his many problems. The relief of finally understanding what happened to him and the camaraderie of being with a group of people who have been through the same experiences fill him with hope and energy. His self-esteem increases and his enthusiasms multiply. For the first time in years, everything seems to be clear and sensible.

After two weeks or so in treatment, the alcoholic often appears to be healed and ready to be released. He understands his disease; he finally admits how sick he was when he was drinking; and he is filled with hope and confidence. He wants to get out and prove to everyone that he can stay sober. This euphoric stage is dangerous, however, for the alcoholic's understanding of his disease is still somewhat superficial and unstable. If he is released now, he will probably relapse. He must go through one final stage if he is to achieve a secure and unshakable sobriety.

> After three days in detox, Barbara was transferred to a room she was to share with two other women. Marie was only 35 and a vice-president of a downtown bank. She voluntarily entered treatment when her boss, a recovered alcoholic, gave her the choice of treatment or losing her job. Joan was a middle-aged housewife, obviously in bad physical and mental shape. Her hands shook constantly and

uncontrollably, she talked to herself when she was awake and asleep, and she cried off and on, day and night.

After hearing her roommates' drinking histories, Barbara still could not accept the fact that she was an alcoholic like them. She looked in the mirror, and there was the proof that she was better off than most everyone else in the treatment center. She looked healthy, perhaps a bit thin with the skin stretched tight over her cheekbones, but she was not anything like Joan, who shook all day and all night, or Bob, the man across the hall who was up every night yelling into the phone to his business partner that they should buy new trucks because the lettuce crop was so successful this year. Barbara told herself that she was not physically handicapped, and she was not mentally fogged. She was just not like the rest of them, she decided.

As the days went by and she began to think more clearly and rationally, Barbara began to examine her past in more detail. She told her counseling group about her suicide attempts, about the psychiatrist who gave her Valium for her depression, about her dancing classes and how she would have to cancel them when she was drinking too much. She thought about her children and the many times they had tried to talk to her about her drinking; after a while, she had stopped talking to them and tried harder to conceal her drinking. She remembered the night her 15-year-old daughter found her in the closet, an empty vodka bottle in her hand and vomit all over her clothes.

She remembered all the parties when she embarrassed her husband by drinking too much.

She remembered that she had stopped going to parties and then drank only at home; she remembered the endless talks when her husband would break down and cry, begging her to stop drinking. She also remembered the last time when he was so cold and stern, and she knew that he meant it when he offered her one last chance.

As she remembered, she slowly accepted the truth. She knew that she could not control her drinking. She realized that alcohol was not her friend but her enemy. Gradually she realized how lucky she was. She had almost lost everything that mattered to her. The realization frightened her, because she had never understood it before. In the past, she thought only of drinking and resented anyone who prevented her from drinking the way she wanted to drink.

She saw the improvement in her roommates. Joan's hands stopped shaking, and Marie began to look as if she might be an attractive woman. Bob laughed at himself now for his crazy nightly phone calls and nearly cried with relief that his partner had not kicked him out of the business.

She saw the looks in her children's eyes when they came to visit her, and she knew in a way that she would never know by looking in the mirror how changed she really was.

She was slowly filled with enthusiasm and hope. She understood her disease, she accepted it, and she actually wanted to live without alcohol. She wanted to stay sane and sober and healthy. She knew she could make it through; she was certain she had the disease licked.

Commitment

Understanding alone cannot reliably keep the alcoholic sober for the long term. Understanding the disease is helpful only if it guides the alcoholic to live differently than he used to live. "You have to walk the walk, not just talk the talk," said alcoholic expert Father Martin, referring to the fact that the alcoholic must do more than talk about his disease and decide to stay sober—he must commit his thoughts and actions to living a life without alcohol.[6] This commitment signifies a total acceptance of the disease and the life style necessary to staying sober.

In this last stage of treatment, the enthusiasm reached during the stage of understanding becomes a committed determination. The belief that "this is going to be a snap" slowly evolves into the knowledge that sobriety is not easily won but requires a new life style with built-in vigilance and protection. Complacency can ruin sobriety, for when the alcoholic is feeling confident and certain of his ability to stay sober, he may loosen his controls, relax his vigilance, and allow himself to "cheat" just a little. He may give in to a craving for sweets; he may work too hard and forget to eat as he should; he may miss A.A. meetings because he does not feel that he needs them anymore; he may think that after months or years of sobriety he can experiment with a drink or two every once in a while; or because he feels completely normal and doesn't crave alcohol, he may decide that he isn't really an alcoholic after all.

The disease may not look so dangerous now that he has been sober for a while. Strict controls may seem unnecessary. He may believe that his years of sobriety have proved his ability to resist temptation. Whatever the reason, if the alcoholic is feeling complacent, his sobriety is in danger, and he must renew his commitment to his program of life-long sobriety.

Most important of all, the alcoholic must accept

the responsibility for his own recovery. If he says "It is going to be really easy for me to stick to my diet because my wife won't let me get away with cheating," or "I won't have any choice but to attend A.A. meetings because my kids will drop me off and wait until the meeting is over," he is placing the future of his sobriety on someone else rather than taking the primary responsibility himself. Whenever an alcoholic's sobriety is dependent on another human being, it is a temporary sobriety because human beings get sick, die, lose patience, fall out of love, or move out of town. An alcoholic who places the responsibility for his sobriety on someone else is jeopardizing his life.

To stay sober, the alcoholic must understand that his susceptibility to addiction will never go away; he must accept the fact that he can never safely take a drink. He must learn everything he can about the disease and then incorporate this knowledge into his life, making a profound, deeply felt commitment to living without alcohol. If he avoids this commitment and hopes that someday he might be able to drink again, he will.

Barbara was ready to be discharged. The fourth and last week in treatment had been difficult and demanding, and she felt a little shaky about being on her own and away from the protection of the hospital. She was afraid she might fail, for she realized now how easy it would be to take a drink.

Her counselor assured her that her fears were a good sign: they showed that she was being realistic about the problems she might face in the immediate future. "Sobriety is like learning to ride a bicycle," he explained. "At first, it is scary and easy to fall off. Yet, after a short while, riding a bike is as easy as walking. But you have to keep going forward, or you will fall over. The trick, then, is not to become complacent and think you are invulnerable. Don't take chances; don't play games. Above all, get to your follow-up meetings and A.A. and stay on your nutritional program."

Barbara realized that she was learning to take responsibility for her own behavior and that this responsibility carried a heavy weight. She understood her disease. She knew that living the program was her protection.

One day shortly before her release, Barbara remembered a teen-age incident involving her diabetic grandmother. She had walked into her grandmother's kitchen to find her nibbling on cookies just from the oven. "Grandmother, you're not allowed to eat those!" she cried. Her grandmother's eyes grew wide, and her mouth trembled in anger. "How can I cook without taking a sample to see if it's good enough for everyone else to eat?" she asked angrily. "Now get out of my kitchen!"

Barbara realized now that her grandmother never completely accepted the chronic and progressive nature of her disease. In the kitchen she cheated whenever she wanted, and her rationalizations and denials made everyone in the family so uncomfortable that they ignored her nibbling. But diabetes, like alcoholism, is lethal, and cheating can be fatal. Barbara's grandmother died in a diabetic coma at the age of 65.

Barbara knew that staying sober would sometimes be difficult, but she also knew one other fact—her life depended on her staying sober. She also knew, through the example of hundreds of thousands of recovered alcoholics that she could do it. And more than anything else in the world, she wanted to stay sober.

"My life began during treatment," Barbara told her counselor the day she left the program. "Before treatment, I was someone else, ruled and controlled by alcohol. But during treatment I saw miracles worked with the other patients, and I realized that the change in my life was also something of a miracle. Now nothing is more important to me than my sobriety—not my husband, my children, or my career—because I would not have them if I started to drink again. If I lose my sobriety, I lose everything."

10

Drugs and the Alcoholic

...a high percentage of alcoholics—some of whom are aware of their drinking problem and try to hide it, and some of whom are not able to recognize it—visit their doctors for tranquilizer prescriptions because their complaints mirror the symptoms of anxiety or stress for which tranquilizers are promoted. These complaints—nervousness, anxiety, insomnia, and so on—sound to some doctors like a classic case of anxiety when they are, in fact, a reflection of the early stages of alcoholism. Doctors are too quick to reach for the prescription pad when they hear such complaints.

Richard Hughes and Robert Brewin,
The Tranquilizing of America

Alcohol in combination with other drugs can be deadly. The case of Karen Ann Quinlan is perhaps the most famous and dramatic example of the killing power of combined drugs. One night in 1974, the 20-year-old Quinlan drank several gin and tonics and took some pills. She lapsed into a coma and years later, with all life-supporting equipment removed, she continued to lie unconscious and unknowing in a New Jersey nursing home.

Cases of drug addiction and overdose among the famous are reported frequently in the news. Elvis

Presley died of an apparent heart attack, although he was taking "uppers," "downers," and mood changers in quantities that would have toppled a horse. Judy Garland and Marilyn Monroe were destroyed by alcohol and prescription drugs. Dorothy Kilgallen died one night after taking moderate doses of alcohol and barbiturates—taken separately, the individual drug doses were not considered dangerous; taken together, they were lethal. Betty Ford, a moderate social drinker for most of her life, became addicted to both alcohol and drugs prescribed by her doctors for a pinched nerve and arthritis.

When celebrities get in trouble with drugs or die of drug/alcohol interactions, the story hits the front page. For each celebrity, however, there are thousands of cases that are never reported or are noted only on the obituary page. Anyone who drinks and takes tranquilizers or sedatives at the same time is toying with a chemical time bomb which could explode into multiple addictions, multiple withdrawal syndromes, convulsions, coma, and death. One drink plus one pill does not equal the effect of two drinks or two pills. Instead, the potency of the drugs is multiplied three times, four times, or even more.

Recent research by Charles Lieber provides at least a partial explanation of why these explosive interactions occur.[1] Lieber found that alcohol and tranquilizing drugs compete for the same enzyme processing system in the liver. This is the system that metabolizes drugs, eventually inactivating them and eliminating them through the blood stream. When alcohol is taken in combination with tranquilizers or other central nervous system depressants, the enzymes are unable to work on both drugs at the same time. Alcohol is always given first priority, and the other drug must, in effect, wait in line for its turn to be processed and eliminated. This delay in normal processing causes the tranquilizing drug's effects to be magnified, since they are allowed to build up and remain active for a longer time.

Alcoholics are in particular danger when combining various drugs because their cells are already chemically altered by long exposure to large doses of alcohol, and these alterations affect the cells' reactions to other drugs. As one researcher explains, the normal drug interactions are changed because the person taking the drugs is changed:

> . . . the interaction is not so much between two drugs as between an organism modified by exposure to one of these drugs (ethanol) and the subsequent modification in the reaction of that organism to some other drug.[2]

This altered interaction is particularly noticeable with tranquilizers, sedatives, and all other drugs which act as central nervous system depressants. When the alcoholic takes these prescription drugs, he experiences an unusual effect—the prescribed drug dose is simply not strong enough. The alcoholic is instantly tolerant to central nervous system depressants because his central nervous system cells are already tolerant to alcohol. Having adapted to one drug, his cells are also adapted to similar drugs, and in order to get the intended effect, he must take more pills than prescribed.

This instantaneous ability to withstand the effects of drugs pharmacologically similar to alcohol is termed *cross-tolerance*. It accounts for the alcoholic's ability to continue to function with tranquilizer or sedative doses, for example, which would be incapacitating or even lethal for nonalcoholics.

The dangers of cross-tolerance are obvious. Because of his increased tolerance, the alcoholic has to drink more to experience the desired effects of alcohol; if he is taking prescription pills, he will also have to increase the dosage to get the intended effect. Combined, these large drug doses are extremely dangerous, even for the alcoholic who can tolerate large doses of each drug individually. As Lieber's research demonstrates, the effects of the tranquilizer or sedative are magnified because alcohol always wins the competition for the enzyme-processing system. The other drug then builds up in the blood stream and can cause toxic reactions including coma, convulsions, and respiratory failure.

Furthermore, a drinking alcoholic on pills is often too befuddled to medicate himself according to directions. He may forget when or if he took his last pill, or he may double or triple the prescribed dose in an attempt to forestall the inevitable withdrawal symptoms. Accidental overdoses are frequent because the alcoholic simply loses track of his intake of pills and alcohol.

For late-stage alcoholics, the dangers of combining pills and alcohol are intensified. As described in chapter 4, chronic exposure to large doses of alcohol weakens the cell membranes and enlarges and distorts the energy-producing cell parts, the mitochondria. As the cells progressively become weaker, they are no longer able to function normally with large doses of alcohol, and the alcoholic's tolerance for alcohol gradually decreases. At the same time, his tolerance for tranquilizers and sedatives decreases as well. The alcoholic is now in an extremely precarious situation if he combines alcohol and prescription drugs, for his tolerance is lessening and yet his withdrawal symptoms are increasing in frequency and intensity as the addiction strengthens. He must continually medicate himself with alcohol and/or pills; yet his weakened cells can no longer tolerate the amounts necessary to stop the physical and mental anguish of withdrawal. Once again, the dangers of accidental overdose are very real.

Disease further weakens the alcoholic's ability to withstand the combined effects of alcohol and prescription pills. An injured liver is incapable of eliminating drugs at a normal rate, and the drug's effects will be enhanced and prolonged. Other alcohol-related diseases including kidney disease, pancreatitis, and gastrointesti-

nal disorders contribute to the body's inability to metabolize and eliminate various drugs.

Not the least of the late-stage alcoholic's problems
is the constant mental confusion and emotional distress
associated with drinking a lot of alcohol over a long
period of time. When the alcoholic is drinking, his
brain is saturated with alcohol, and he cannot think
straight or reason rationally. When he is not drinking,
he is in withdrawal, and his thoughts are equally confused and jumbled. As a result, he spends most of his
waking hours confused, in pain from withdrawal,
overwhelmed with self-pity and despair, and often depressed beyond all caring. Swallowing a bottle of pills
may seem the only way to escape a hopeless, miserable
existence.

While the phenomenon of *cross-tolerance* helps
explain some of the dangers associated with combining
alcohol and prescription drugs, it does not explain why
hundreds of thousands of alcoholics become addicted to
prescription drugs. Are these alcoholics, in fact, addictive personalities, or is there some physiological explanation for the alcoholic's increased susceptibility to
multiple addiction?

As with most of the mysteries in alcoholism, the
explanation is physiological, not psychological. Addiction to alcohol ensures that the alcoholic will quickly
become addicted to pharmacologically similar drugs, a
process called *cross-addiction*. Tranquilizers and sedatives are addictive for anyone who uses them over a
long period of time, even if they are taken as prescribed.
For alcoholics, however, the drug addiction process is
speeded up. Since the alcoholic's cells are already physically addicted to alcohol, the cellular equipment necessary for addiction to tranquilizers and sedatives, is, in a
sense, already established.

Because these drugs can partially substitute for
alcohol in relieving withdrawal symptoms, because the

symptoms of alcoholism mirror emotional disorders, and because many physicians are not aware of the cross-addiction process in alcoholics, sedatives and tranquilizers are often prescribed for alcoholics, with instructions to use them whenever they feel shaky, nervous, or anxious. While the alcoholic may feel better temporarily after taking a sedative or tranquilizer, he will rapidly become addicted to the drug if he continues to take it.

Once addicted to both alcohol and prescription drugs, the alcoholic experiences a complex combination of withdrawal symptoms, and his mental and physical torment multiplies. The dual or multiply addicted alcoholic is caught in a brutal cycle of increasing pain and decreasing benefits, as he must step up his use of alcohol or pills to medicate himself against the ever-impending and increasingly severe withdrawal symptoms. Blackouts, mental confusion, and suicidal depressions intensify with multiple addictions, and the possibility of overdose dramatically increases.

A critical and dangerously overlooked aspect of addiction to alcohol and/or drugs is its permanence. Once established, the addiction can be reactivated by using either alcohol or prescription drugs, even after prolonged periods of abstinence. Tranquilizers and sedatives, for example, because of their similar effects to alcohol on the central nervous system can reactivate the physical addiction to alcohol, causing a craving for alcohol which leads to a return to drinking.[3] Many sober alcoholics given medication for tension, pain, or insomnia have relapsed and started drinking again. Over-the-counter medications containing alcohol, such as cough syrup, also can and do trigger the addiction and start a sober alcoholic drinking again.

As Betty Ford's ordeal with pills and alcohol demonstrates, even moderate nonalcoholic drinkers can become addicted to alcohol if they are simultaneously taking prescription drugs. For years, Betty Ford had been a social drinker who was also taking pills prescribed by her doctors for pain and stress. "I had never been without my drugs," she confides in her autobiography, *The Times of My Life*. "I took pills for pain, I took pills to sleep, I took mild tranquilizers."[4] At some point, however, her body was no longer able to tolerate the combination of prescription drugs and alcohol. She began to slur her words, stumble on the stairs, and behave in ways totally unlike herself. With no warning, she had become addicted to both pills and alcohol.

In actuality, the addiction process had probably been established years before, but her doctors never detected the addiction, and she therefore had no reason to suspect it. The pills were prescribed for legitimate complaints, and she took them as directed—how could they be dangerous? She drank alcohol, but no one ever warned her not to, and she rarely drank to excess—how could she be an alcoholic? Her bewilderment is reflected in the following passage from her autobiography:

> The reason I rejected the idea that I was an alcoholic was that my addiction wasn't dramatic. So I forgot a few telephone calls. So I fell in the bathroom and cracked three ribs. But I never drank for a hangover, and in fact, I used to criticize people who did. At house parties, I would look at friends who knocked back Bloody Marys in the morning, and I would think, isn't that pathetic?
>
> I hadn't been a solitary drinker, either; I'd never hidden bottles in the chandeliers or the toilet tanks. When Jerry was away, there had always been neighbors to have cocktails with, either at their houses or at our house, and at Washington luncheons I'd never touched anything but an occasional glass of sherry. There had been no broken promises (my husband

never came to me and said, "Please quit") and no drunken driving. I worried about my children too much to risk taking them anywhere in a car when I'd been drinking. And I never wound up in jail, or in a strange part of town with a bunch of sailors.[5]

Yet Betty Ford was addicted to pills and alcohol. Millions of Americans have suffered the same fate. Alcoholic treatment centers throughout the country report that over half of their patients are addicted to both alcohol and one or more prescription drugs. What can only be termed a multiple-addiction epidemic has swept the country, and it has hit women particularly hard. The National Institute on Drug Abuse (NIDA) estimates that 32 million women—or 42 percent of the adult female population—have taken tranquilizers at some time in their lives; 21 percent (16 million) have used other prescription sedatives, and 16 percent (12 million) have used stimulants. One of every five women, or 16 million women 18 years and older, take tranquilizers in any given year; of these women, the Food and Drug Administration estimates that two in five, or 6.5 million, are regular users of alcohol and one in five, or more than 3.2 million, is a heavy user.[6]

That these figures add up to a major problem is evident in a 1977 survey conducted by Alcoholics Anonymous. In this survey, 29 percent of all women in A.A. reported dual drug addiction; 55 percent of all women under 30 reported multiple addictions to prescription tranquilizers and alcohol.[7]

Like Betty Ford, most "prescription junkies," as they are sometimes called, are normal and healthy before they start taking pills. Their complaints are minor or temporary, and time alone would probably straighten out most of their problems. But physicians give them drugs, they willingly follow doctor's orders and the directions on the pill bottle, and they innocently get hooked. Thus, many people are destroyed, not by any primary illness, but by treatment.

When a patient requests medication, even the knowledgeable and aware physician is presented with a dilemma: Should he probe into the patient's reasons for wanting a tranquilizer and take a detailed medical history to ensure that the patient is not taking or addicted to other medications or alcohol, and should he then spend ten to fifteen minutes explaining the various drug interactions? Or should he simply comply with his patient's request, trusting him to know about the hazards of drug interactions? This dilemma is summed up by Dr. Joseph Cruse, a member of the board of directors of the National Council on Alcoholism:

> I'm amazed at how often I go through the questioning, the examination, and treatment program for the chief complaint, and just before leaving, the patient says "Oh, by the way, Dr. Brown gives me Valium, but he's out of town. Would you write me a prescription for 100?" She is as uncomfortable about asking as I am about refusing. It takes 30 seconds to write the prescription and 30 minutes not to. Now I have to make a hard choice on a busy afternoon when I'm already behind schedule.[8]

When the alcoholic visits a doctor, his complaints frequently appear to be psychological. He can't sleep; his marriage seems to be falling apart; he no longer cares about his work; he is depressed, easily frustrated, and constantly tense. Unless a physician is familiar with the disease of alcoholism and the early, often confusing psychological symptoms, he may not even guess that there is an underlying physical disease which is causing these complaints. The patient is complaining of relatively minor problems which appear to be signs of some kind of temporary difficulty in his social life or career, and the physician may easily misinterpret the symptoms as evidence of a purely emotional or psychological disturbance. The most logical therapy will therefore often appear to be prescription drugs.

When the symptoms persist and increase in intensity—which they will if the alcoholic continues to drink and/or take pills—the physician may increase the dosage or switch his patient to a stronger tranquilizer or sedative. Even with intensified symptoms, there may still be no direct evidence of serious damage to the patient's physical health. In fact, the early alcoholic often appears to be in good physical condition, and a brief medical examination will detect no evidence of organ or tissue damage. Without this evidence, prescription pills again may seem to be the most logical method of treatment.

Even physicians who know a patient's history of heavy drinking may prescribe drugs as part of treatment on the premise that alcoholism is essentially an emotional illness and that drugs are more effective and safer than alcohol in relieving emotional problems. The physician may also hope that his patient can be helped to switch from excessive, uncontrolled drinking to a medically controlled program of drug treatment. The physician may reason that if the alcoholic continues to drink to excess, he will inevitably deteriorate, ending up in prison, a mental institution, or the morgue. If, on the other hand, the patient can be persuaded to switch to prescription drugs, the dosage can at least be controlled.

All of these reasons for using drug therapy are misguided and based on ignorance of both alcoholism and the complex interactions of various drugs. Tranquilizers and sedatives may temporarily alleviate the alcoholic's discomfort, but they will not halt the addiction to alcohol. In fact, they aggravate the addiction and make it even more difficult for the alcoholic to recover. As discussed earlier in this chapter, these drugs speed up the addictive process, increase the risk of accidental overdose and toxic reactions, aggravate the alcoholic's emotional and psychological problems, and cause multiple addictions and multiple withdrawal symptoms. When a physician writes an alcoholic a prescription for a tranquilizer or sedative, he may, in effect, be signing the patient's death certificate.

Writing a prescription for any patient is a heavy responsibility. The physician should, of course, take a detailed medical history before he prescribes drugs, and he should expend some time and energy trying to determine the precise causes of the patient's anxiety or depression. If he decides to prescribe, he should inform the patient about the known and suspected risks associated with taking the drug. He can help protect his patients by using a prescription form which lists the common interactions of drugs and alcohol. Such a form has already been proposed by the National Clearinghouse for Alcohol Information.*

For the alcoholic patients, the physician's responsibilities are even clearer and more straightforward: *Tranquilizers and sedatives should never be prescribed for a known or suspected alcoholic.*

What about Antabuse?

F. Scott Fitzgerald once complained that he could never stay sober long enough to tolerate sobriety. Researchers familiar with this common complaint have long been inspired to search for a substance that would discourage spontaneous drinking and force the alcoholic to stay sober long enough to let rationality prevail.

There is such a substance, but as will be shown, it is a mixed blessing. Antabuse—generically known as

---

*See Appendix D for a copy of this form.

disulfiram—was accidentally discovered when workers in a rubber factory found that they could not drink without becoming violently ill. Shortly after World War II, Danish researchers traced the source of the trouble to tetraethyliuram disulfide, a chemical used in the processing of rubber. In the late 1940s, the chemical was first introduced for use in treating alcoholism.

Alcoholics maintained on Antabuse take a pill every day. As long as the alcoholic abstains from drinking, this daily dose allegedly has no side effect. Just a few minutes after ingesting even small amounts of alcohol, however, a violent reaction occurs. The amount of alcohol in a dose of cough syrup or an alcohol rubdown is enough to initiate this reaction. As described in the *Physician's Desk Reference*, this reaction

> . . . produces flushing, throbbing in head and neck, throbbing headache, respiratory difficulty, nausea, copious vomiting, sweating, thirst, chest pain, palpitation, dyspnea [labored or difficult breathing], hyperventilation, tachycardia [abnormally rapid heart rate], hypotension [low blood pressure], syncope [sudden loss of strength], marked uneasiness, weakness, vertigo, blurred vision and confusion. In severe reactions there may be respiratory depression, cardiovascular collapse, arrhythmias, myocardial infarction, acute congestive heart failure, unconsciousness, convulsions, and death.
>
> The intensity of the reaction varies with each individual, but is generally proportional to the amounts of Antabuse and alcohol ingested.[9]

Antabuse works by interfering with the metabolism of alcohol in the liver. Apparently, the drug stalls metabolism at the acetaldehyde stage so that acetaldehyde accumulates in the body, producing the violent symptoms of the reaction. Because Antabuse is slowly absorbed and excreted, a single dose will "protect" the alcoholic for five to seven days.

While researchers understand the basics of Antabuse's activities in the body, the subtleties of its actions are still being discovered. When the chemical was first used in the 1940s, research on its side effects was almost nonexistent. Human alcoholics were the first guinea pigs, the side effects were noted as they occurred, and dosage was adjusted through trial and error. Over thirty years later, the experimentation continues. Recent findings show that daily doses of Antabuse can have profound effects on the physical and mental health of even the abstinent alcoholic:

- A May 1979 article in the Journal of Studies on Alcohol discusses an early study showing that as many as one-sixth of the people taking Antabuse may become psychotic. Although the incidence of Antabuse-induced psychosis has been reduced significantly with the lower dosages now used, depression and mania remain possibilities during Antabuse therapy and psychotic symptoms can develop in certain "predisposed" patients. [10]
- Seizure activity has been reported in alcoholics who take Antabuse. Researchers hypothesize that the drug interferes with oxygen use in the central nervous system. [11]
- Fetal limb reductions and abnormalities have been linked to the use of Antabuse in pregnant women. [12]
- Because Antabuse inhibits the actions of many enzymes in the human body, it can alter the metabolism of various common drugs and interfere with their metabolism. Anticoagulant drugs combined with Antabuse can cause increased bleeding. Sedatives, tranquilizers, and barbiturates in combination with Antabuse can cause dizziness, nausea, mental confusion, sluggishness, and severe anxiety. [13]

- The toxic effects of Antabuse may occur in almost every organ system. Overdoses may result in various nervous diseases characterized by involuntary, irregular movements and Parkinsonism, a progressive disease of the brain. In addition, the long-term administration of Antabuse may be associated with an increased incidence of arteriosclerotic cardiovascular disease.[14]
- Antabuse may interfere with the liver's normal detoxification processes, thereby enhancing or altering the toxic effects of environmental chemicals. Many alcoholics maintained on Antabuse who are exposed to chemicals at work or at home may thus be at high risk of toxic reactions.[15]
- All medicines containing alcohol, notably over-the-counter cough syrups, will trigger the Antabuse reaction, as will foods prepared with wine or other beverage alcohol.

Clearly, Antabuse is a drug which must be used with extreme caution. The alcoholic's medical history must be taken in detail, and the risks associated with using the drug should be thoroughly outlined. The patient must be made aware of all drugs and foods to avoid, and his physician should regularly monitor him for adverse reactions. Alcoholics with a history of congestive heart failure, liver and kidney disorders, diabetes, thyroid problems, brain damage, polyneuropathy, psychosis, or suicidal tendencies should not be given Antabuse.

The fundamental question, of course, is this: Are the benefits worth the risks? On the positive side, the urge to drink can come over a sober alcoholic suddenly and sweepingly; with Antabuse, he has a means to combat this urge and to give himself time to think rationally. Antabuse can buy precious time.

Yet while Antabuse may temporarily deter some alcoholics from impulse drinking, it does little or nothing to ensure or promote life-long sobriety. Antabuse cannot control or eliminate the physical addiction to alcohol, a fact underscored by the many patients who simply stop taking their daily Antabuse when the craving for alcohol asserts itself. Tragically, the physical imperative to drink may be much more powerful than fear of the Antabuse reaction, and the alcoholic may then drink while taking Antabuse and suffer the dangerous and sometimes fatal consequences.

Finally, and also on the negative side, the use of Antabuse can distract the alcoholic from assuming responsibility for staying sober. The alcoholic is depending on a drug to keep him sober, and once the drug is removed, he will very likely start drinking again.

The alcoholic's continued sobriety depends, to a large extent, on his ability to come to grips with the chronic nature of his disease. He must understand that his vulnerability to alcohol's harmful effects will not go away with time, and he must therefore continually guard against potential obstacles or hazards to his sobriety. With effective treatment, this need not be a grim and constant struggle. When an alcoholic learns the facts of his disease, he will know why he cannot drink and what to do to protect his sobriety. When the deficiencies in his nutrition have been corrected, the recurring bouts of depression, anxiety, and craving for alcohol will subside.

As a general rule, then, Antabuse can be used, under medical supervision, for some alcoholics as a temporary aid in the first weeks or months of sobriety, when the risks of relapse are highest. With the advent of effective treatment, however, the alcoholic will not need to rely on Antabuse to keep him sober. The power to say "no" to alcohol will come from within and not from a chemical prison imposed from without.

11

Beyond Prejudice
and Misconception

*He that is possessed with a prejudice is possessed
with a devil, and one of the worst kind of devils, for
it shuts out the truth, and often leads to grievous
error.*

Tryon Edwards

It is never too late to give up your prejudices.

Henry David Thoreau, *Walden*

The information in this book can save millions of
lives and billions of dollars, but first, two types of
prejudice must be destroyed. Prejudice born of ignorance is fairly easily won over once the facts are made
available and people are given accurate information.
Prejudice born of interest is not so easily destroyed,
however, for the facts can be misinterpreted, denied, or
covered up. Those who have a professional or economic
need to view alcoholism as a mental health problem will
cling stubbornly to their prejudices, ignoring or slanting
the evidence. They will not be able to see the facts or
accept them, for the facts disorder their particular view
of the world.

The prejudice of vested interests is epidemic in the

field of alcoholism. The federal government supplies millions of dollars every year for alcoholism research, treatment, education, and prevention. The competition for these funds is stiff, and the stakes are high—an atmosphere perfectly suited to the breeding of hostility, jealousy, and carefully guarded self-interest.

The battle against the prejudices of ignorance and interest will eventually be won—the facts themselves will tip the scales—but it will not happen overnight. It may take years for society to slough off the myths and misconceptions concerning alcoholism that have governed thought for centuries. But it will happen. Every recovered alcoholic adds fuel to the fire of this movement forward. Doctors who are trained and educated in early diagnosis and treatment, employers who offer the alcoholic the choice of treatment instead of automatically firing him, family members who witness the recovery process, and policemen, lawyers, judges, and social workers who come in contact with recovered alcoholics and effective treatment programs all help to advance the new understanding of alcoholism. As researchers contribute to the already substantial body of evidence, as effective treatment programs replace ineffective ones, and as the number of recovered alcoholics enjoying lasting sobriety continues to grow, this movement will gain a momentum which cannot be stopped.

It can—and must—be accelerated, however. Major overhauls must take place in all areas of alcoholism. These changes cannot be superficial but must be deep, massive alterations in the social, political, and economic fabric of this country as it relates to alcoholism. The changes required are so sweeping that an entire book could be devoted solely to outlining and exploring them. The following survey is therefore intended only to highlight those areas which require immediate and significant change.

The Need for Definitions

Each of us has his private view and private meaning attached to the words that are used in the alcohol field.[1]

Universally accepted definitions do not exist in the alcoholism field. As the researcher quoted above acknowledges, everyone involved in the field has his own private view of the disease. The professionals believe they are entitled to their own opinions about alcoholism because there has been, until now, no clear picture of what alcoholism is, what causes it, how it progresses, and why certain people become addicted while others do not.

And yet, as this book makes clear, there is a firm basis of research evidence for understanding the disease. The disease itself is understandable and definable; the victim's behavior is understandable and definable; and the recovery process is understandable and definable.

Opinions must no longer be allowed to overshadow facts. An example of the dangers inherent in allowing researchers to interpret the data according to their own private meanings is contained in a 1976 Rand Report. In this government-funded study, which assessed the effectiveness of forty-four federal government treatment programs, the term "recovery" was replaced with a broader term "remission." "Remission" included the category "normal drinking," defined by the authors as drinking less than 3 ounces of pure alcohol every day.[2] An alcoholic was considered to be in remission, then, if he was drinking the equivalent of 6 ounces or less of 100 proof whiskey every day. Thus, treatment centers which embraced this definition of "remission" could claim up to 80 percent success rates—even though most of the alcoholics so labelled were still drinking.

The word "remission" by itself is not offensive, but when it is used to describe acceptable "normal drinking" in alcoholics, the dangers are very real. The Rand Report created an uproar in the field of alcoholism when it was published, with some professionals insisting that the report provided evidence that some alcoholics could return to normal drinking, and others condemning the study as dangerous and irresponsible since it might encourage alcoholics to believe that they could control their drinking permanently.

Four years later, the Rand researchers backed away from their original conclusions. A follow-up study found that the so-called normal alcoholic drinkers had nearly three times the relapse rate of long-term abstainers when they tried to stop drinking. "Normal drinking" is clearly not possible for the alcoholic; while he can control his intake for a period of months or even years, his disease will steadily progress until eventually the addiction overpowers his best efforts to control it.

Another example of the power of words to promote misconception is the use of the term "alcohol abuse" as a synonym for "alcoholism." "Alcohol abuse" identifies alcoholism as a compulsion, like overeating or gambling, and puts the onus on the person who allegedly abuses the substance. Because the term cannot encompass the ideas that alcoholism is a disease and that alcoholics are innocent victims, the result has been the development of a theory that two types of alcoholism exist: one a physical disease, and the other a compulsive, psychologically caused abuse of alcohol. The National Institute on Alcohol Abuse and Alcoholism by its very name gives support to this contradictory view of alcoholism.

The need for precise definitions should be obvious. The following definitions, based on the facts already established in the scientific literature, are central to any attempt to communicate clearly about alcoholism.

Alcoholism. A chronic, primary, hereditary disease which progresses from an early, physiological suscepti- bility into an addiction characterized by tolerance changes, physiological dependence, and loss of control over drinking. Psychological symptoms are secondary to the physiological disease and not relevant to its onset.

Recovery. A return to normal functioning based on total, continuous abstinence from alcohol and substitute drugs, corrective nutrition, and an accurate understand- ing of the disease. The word "cure" should not be used because it implies that the alcoholic can engage in normal drinking after his "problem" has been corrected.

Problem Drinker. A person who is not an alcoholic but whose alcohol use creates psychological and social problems for himself and/or others.

Heavy Drinker. Anyone who drinks frequently or in large amounts. A heavy drinker may be a problem drinker, an alcoholic, or a normal drinker with a high tolerance for alcohol.

Alcoholic. An alcoholic is a person with the disease of alcoholism regardless of whether he is initially a heavy drinker, a problem drinker, or a light or moderate drinker. The alcoholic's increasing problems and his heavier drinking stem from his addiction and should not be confused with problem drinking or heavy drinking in the nonalcoholic.

Recovered Alcoholic. The alcoholic who maintains continuous, total abstinence from alcohol and substitute drugs and who has returned to a normal life style. The term "reformed alcoholic" implies that the alcoholic has been "bad" and is now being "good"—a reflection of the moralistic approach to alcoholism which has no basis in fact. The term "ex-alcoholic" should not be used either, for it implies a cure rather than a recovery.

Relapse ("Slip" in A.A. language). Any intake of alcohol or substitute drug by a recovering alcoholic. The taking of a substitute drug, although not usually considered a relapse, seriously interferes with recovery and almost always leads to a return to drinking.

Research Priorities

Researchers have already provided an abundance of knowledge about the disease of alcoholism, including its onset, underlying mechanisms, predisposing factors, symptoms, and progression. In particular, the work of Charles Lieber on the metabolism of alcohol, Benjamin Kissin on the causes and progression of the disease, Roger Williams on hypoglycemia and nutrition, Donald Goodwin on heredity, and Bert Vallee on liver enzyme activities have provided notable milestones in understanding alcoholism.

Because much of the major ground-breaking work has been accomplished, researchers can now direct their efforts to adding important knowledge within this general framework. It is particularly important, however, that they be precise about what they are studying and measuring. For example, they should be sure to make these distinctions: Is the drinker an alcoholic, or is he a heavy drinker or a problem drinker? Is the alcoholic in the early, middle, or late stages of his disease? Is the alcoholic in acute withdrawal or protracted withdrawal? Is alcohol responsible for the effect observed, is acetaldehyde responsible, or are both substances contributing? Is the drinker experiencing the direct effects of alcohol or the effects of the withdrawal of alcohol?

Areas for further refinement of knowledge would include the following:

Nutrition. The role of nutrition in the onset and progression of alcoholism, the withdrawal syndrome, and the treatment and recovery process has been neglected, and the whole range of disciplines—biochemistry, pharmacology, physiology—should thoroughly explore this clinically important area.

Drug Interactions. Another fertile area for research by the life scientists is drug interactions. Particular areas of interest are the addictive properties of drugs in the alcoholic whether or not he is drinking, the long-term or cumulative effects of taking various drugs, the special problems created by dual addiction, and so on.

Heredity. The evidence is overwhelming that alcoholism is a hereditary disease. Replication and extension of research findings is needed here, particularly in the area of identifying the specific genetic factors that predispose persons to alcoholism.

Enzyme Abnormalities. Fortunately, numerous competent researchers are advancing knowledge in this area. Work such as Vallee's at Harvard Medical School, for example, should further clarify the specific liver enzymes involved in alcoholism. The potential significance of this research is enormous and should be encouraged by both public and private funding.

Acetaldehyde. The complex relationships between alcohol, acetaldehyde, and other breakdown products needs continued attention.

Protracted Withdrawal Syndrome. Kissin and others have laid the groundwork for understanding the source of the recovering alcoholic's continued psychological and social problems. The linkage between psychological problems and their physiological causes is a key area in the study of alcoholism and should receive continued strong support.

Fetal Alcohol Syndrome. One of the more exciting areas of study is the effect of alcohol on the fetus. Future research should identify the amounts of alcohol and frequency of drinking that endanger the fetus. Education and prevention efforts can then identify the specific women at risk and offer sound, sensible advice on drinking habits during pregnancy.

Education and Prevention

Education efforts in the past have circulated misinformation as fast as factual knowledge. For example, the federal government spent millions of dollars promoting the idea that alcohol abuse causes alcoholism and that responsible drinking will prevent it. This "responsible drinking" campaign cultivated the belief that alcoholism is a symptom of psychological and social problems rather than a physiological disease.

One of the most controversial issues in alcoholism education today is whether or not the federal government should put warning labels on alcoholic beverages. Proponents insist that people should be warned about the health hazards associated with drinking alcohol and that labelling is both useful and less costly than other forms of government action. Yet moderate alcohol comsumption is not hazardous for most people, and the health risks related to drinking alcohol are different for different people. Pregnant women and people taking various medications, for example, are at a higher risk of adverse effects from even moderate amounts of alcohol. Furthermore, the focus on alcohol itself only confuses the issue and misses the main target, which is the biologically susceptible individual. The alcoholic may read the label, but it will make little or no difference in how much he drinks; his drinking is regulated by his addiction, and his psychological control over this addiction lessens dramatically as the disease progresses. Nonalcoholics, on the other hand, may simply be annoyed by the warning label, as their drinking behavior is usually not a threat to themselves or to others.

Future education efforts must shift focus and concentrate on identifying those individuals who should temporarily avoid or cut down on their drinking—pregnant women, for example—and those individuals who are at risk for alcoholism—that is, those in certain ethnic groups and in families with a high incidence of alcoholism. Educational efforts should then be directed to explaining why these individuals are at risk and precisely what the risks are. Low risk individuals—the majority of drinkers—should also be educated about the disease and its early symptoms so that they can make the right decision when confronted with alcoholics at home, at work, or at social gatherings. With accurate information, both groups can make sensible decisions.

Factual knowledge about alcoholism must be the foundation of any prevention effort. Federal programs in the past have been based on the misconception that alcoholism is a behavior-based problem with psychological, social, and cultural roots, and thus prevention efforts have been weak or even counter-productive. One example of misguided prevention efforts was the approval of a $1.5 million federal grant to Eskimo villages where alcoholism rates ran as high as 70 percent.[3] The money was earmarked to build village recreational centers, which would, it was hoped, ease the villagers' boredom and isolation and thus cut down on the amount they drink. But boredom is not a cause of alcoholism, and while the Eskimo villagers may need and use the recreation centers, these centers will not have any significant impact on alcoholism rates. What the villagers really need is accurate information about the disease and comprehensive treatment.

Alcoholism prevention programs should be directed at attacking and halting the physical disease. Comprehensive educational programs and effective treatment centers should clearly be the cornerstones of these programs.

The New Professionals

Aside from research, credit for most of the progress in the field of alcoholism belongs to men and women with specialized education and training, who are dedicated to helping the alcoholic recover. Most are recovered alcoholics, but in recent years, a growing number of nonalcoholics have joined their ranks, usually men and women whose own lives have been touched by alcoholism in their families.*

Tens of thousands of these new professionals, like an underground army, have manned the battle stations on all fronts and at all echelons in the fight against alcoholism. They have spearheaded important federal and state legislation, staffed the burgeoning treatment and rehabilitation programs, and provided the primary liaison between the established agencies and professions and the still sick alcoholic. Though often successful, their work has been difficult and frustrating because of the lack of a coherent understanding of alcoholism. By accepting the false premise that alcoholism is caused by character flaws and personality problems, they invited endless jurisdictional and administrative conflicts with mental health professionals and community agencies which view alcoholism as secondary to psychological

---

*With the formation of the National Association of Alcoholism Counselors (founded in 1972 under a different name), the new professionals are finding a unified voice in the field of alcoholism.

and social problems. Most of the educational and training centers for these new professionals in alcoholism perpetuate this error. By accepting alcoholism as a primary, physiological disease, the role of these professional alcoholism counselors will be clarified and enhanced, and they can become a real force in instituting the new understanding of alcoholism.

Physician Education and Training

Physicians in the past have received little or no training in alcoholism in medical school; most do not have the experience or the skills to recognize or diagnose alcoholism in its early stages; and the majority have scant familiarity with available treatment methods, with A.A., or with the current scientific literature on the subject.

The primary reason for this neglect is that the medical profession, along with the rest of society, has classified alcoholism as a psychological disorder. Physicians routinely treat the more serious physical consequences of alcoholism, that is, liver, heart, and respiratory disease, but often miss the underlying cause—the alcoholism itself. To the extent that physicians do recognize alcoholism, it is usually as a symptom of psychological and social problems beyond their area of expertise and responsibility.

Joseph Pursch, an outspoken critic of the medical profession and a physician himself, has long and loudly insisted that physician ignorance about alcoholism and prejudice toward alcoholics are the major obstacles to effective treatment. At the August 1978 meeting of the National Association of Alcoholism Counselors (NAAC), Pursch emphasized the importance of educating the physician: "The best thing you can do," he told the counselors, "is to decrease the ignorance and increase the awareness and knowledge of physicians." One of the most effective means of changing the physician's attitude toward the alcoholic, Pursch continued, is to emphasize the fact that alcoholism is a treatable disease and that alcoholics by the thousands get well every year. "It's quite remarkable that the healers of the country don't know anyone who is getting well from alcoholism—which means that they only know those who are dying." Pursch went on to explain that this continuing view of alcoholics as hopeless and their disease as inevitably fatal helps to prejudice the doctor's view and reinforce his desire not to treat alcoholics.[4]

In recent years, several programs have finally begun to address the problem of educating physicians about alcoholism. In 1978, for example, Dartmouth Medical School received a $250,000 grant from Operation Cork, a national education program, to develop a model for integrating the study of alcohol and alcoholism into existing medical school courses. In 1980, five medical schools—Case Western Reserve in Cleveland, University of Colorado in Denver, Morehouse College in Atlanta, Rush Medical College in Chicago, and the University of Washington in Seattle—joined with Dartmouth to form the Cork Consortium. Each school will receive $50,000 to initiate curriculum changes in the study of alcoholism.[5]

And yet the Cork Consortium is one small step in what must be a massive effort. To be maximally effective, the content of physician education and training programs must be based on the understanding that alcoholism is a physiological disease and not a symptom of psychological, social, or cultural problems. Once the medical profession accepts this basic point, they can very quickly understand the techniques and skills appropriate to their role in helping alcoholics recover.

The Role of Psychiatry

Psychiatrists virtually controlled the alcoholism field for many years, holding the top posts in NIAAA and other funding agencies, receiving major research grants, and helping to shape the general public opinion of alcoholism as a mental health problem with a psychological and emotional roots.

In the past ten years or so, however, the "mental health" view of alcoholism has come under increasing attack. Psychiatrists have gradually been phased out of positions of leadership in federal, state and local alcoholism programs, and larger chunks of the available research money have been funneled from psychiatry into the biological and neurophysiological sciences. New leaders in the field, influenced by the abundance of research showing that alcoholism is a physiological disease, have suggested that psychiatry, by ignoring or downplaying the physiological aspects and concentrating instead on the superficial psychological symptoms, may even harm the patient by delaying treatment, increasing his guilt and shame, and allowing him to deny his drinking problem or blame it on someone or something else. The following comments illustrate the changing attitudes:

- In 1973, NIAAA Deputy Director Kenneth Eaton told a special task force that alcoholism is "not a mental health problem," adding that the psychiatric approach to alcoholism is "not only the most expensive, but probably the least effective."
- Peter Bourne, M.D., President Jimmy Carter's Special Assistant for Health Issues and a psychiatrist himself, told a December 9, 1977, board meeting of the Alcohol and Drug Problems Association (ADPA) that "one of the big battles you are going to face in the next few

years is whether psychiatrists should have any involvement at all in treating people with alcoholism problems."
He predicted that this battle would be resolved in
favor of the "non-psychiatric position as the primary
treatment persons for the alcoholic."

- In January 1978, Peter Brock, then Director of Education and Research for the Group Health Association of
America, reported to the President's Commission on
Mental Health: "Too frequently in the past, the mental
health professionals have approached the alcoholic patient with the idea that if his aberrational behavior
were corrected, his drinking would go away. They
have not addressed the underlying problem, and have
struck out."

- Psychiatrist David Ohlms gave a pointed warning to
psychiatrists and mental health practitioners at the
June 8, 1979, midcentral regional meeting of the
National Association of Alcoholism Counselors:

> . . . as long as the mental health field insists on
> viewing alcoholism as a symptom rather than a
> primary disease that creates its own symptoms,
> it should keep its nose out of this [alcoholism]
> field.[6]

Underlying the revolt against psychiatric treatment
of alcoholism is the accumulation of evidence that it
simply does not work. Research reports attest to
psychiatry's failure, and many individual psychiatrists
openly admit to it. In a survey of members of the
Southern California Psychiatric Association, for example,
over one-half of the psychiatrists who treated alcoholics
reported no success with any of their alcoholic patients;
for the remainder, success occurred in only 10 percent
of their cases.[7]

The reason that psychiatric treatment does not
work, of course, is that alcoholism is not primarily a

psychological disease. Once psychiatrists understand the physiological bases of the disease, their role will change dramatically. They can learn to diagnose alcoholism as alcoholism—not as a symptom of something else—and they can help to usher patients into the alcoholism recovery sequence. The pioneering efforts of individual psychiatrists such as David Ohlms, Peter Bourne, and Joseph Pursch illustrate the fact that this transformation is not only possible but can be enormously productive for both patients and psychiatrists.

Alcoholics Anonymous

The worldwide organization of A.A. has saved hundreds of thousands of lives, spurred research, and given hope where there was none. But even this remarkable fellowship can improve. In the past, A.A. has been able to change and adapt with the times, a quality which has allowed the organization to expand and grow, reaching ever increasing numbers of alcoholics. As professionals correct their understanding of alcoholism with factual knowledge, A.A. can be expected to adapt its philosophy as well.

A redefinition of the disease, as suggested in this book, will have a profound effect on the A.A. understanding of alcoholism. As a result, character flaws and personality defects will be seen as symptoms of the disease rather than causes, the use of sweets as a substitute for alcohol will be discontinued, and individual A.A. members will be able to work even more effectively with an enlightened professional community. The goal, of course, is not to change the basic structure of A.A. but to expand its unquestionable strengths.

Legal System

The whole approach to alcoholism in the legal system should be transformed. In the absence of a uniform understanding of alcoholism, the fifty states have gone fifty different directions. With a clearer understanding of the disease, more rational legal codes and procedures can be developed. For example, the courts can establish a diagnosis and referral system for alcoholics which will help them avoid the "revolving door" of legal and social agencies and instead help get them into effective treatment. Juvenile laws can recognize that delinquent behavior, including drinking, is often a symptom of the underlying disease of alcoholism rather than a symptom of psychological problems. When the cause is identified, the juvenile offender can be helped into effective treatment. Adult offenders must also be helped. Of adults in prison, an estimated 50 percent are there because of alcohol-related crimes. Yet these prisoners are rarely diagnosed as alcoholics and receive no treatment for their disease. A truly effective criminal justice system would go beyond mere punishment and make effective alcoholism treatment a requirement of parole or probation.

Industry

One of the areas of greatest activity in alcoholism treatment today is employee alcoholism programs (EAPs). Unfortunately, the same old problem plagues this area, namely, the mistaking of alcoholism as a symptom of psychological and social problems. As a consequence, alcoholics are often misdiagnosed and referred to inappropriate or inadequate treatment programs. With a new understanding of alcoholism, however, the EAPs could become far more effective, with the potential of reaching millions of alcoholics.

Insurance

Many insurance policies cover in-patient treatment for alcoholics. However, because of the traditionally low quality of many of these programs, a growing movement favors out-patient treatment and briefer in-patient stays. This trend should be discouraged. Alcoholism is not a self-inflicted illness deserving only minimum care, but a very serious physiological disease fully deserving the best in medical protection and treatment. With improvements in the quality of treatment, it should become clear that effective inpatient treatment is far and away the most cost effective.

The National Institute on Alcohol Abuse and Alcoholism (NIAAA)

In 1970, the National Institute on Alcohol Abuse and Alcoholism (NIAAA) was established in the federal government as a separate agency on the same level as the National Institute on Mental Health (NIMH) and the National Institute on Drug Abuse (NIDA). It is important to understand, however, that NIAAA was established, not to recognize alcoholism as a separate, primary disease, but merely to give alcoholism "more visibility" in the competition for funds.*

Because it has been the greatest source of funds in the alcoholism field, NIAAA has also had the most

---

*With this as the only justification for NIAAA's separate status, the agency will probably be merged back into NIMH or NIDA once visibility has been achieved.

powerful role in shaping programs, public policies, and opinion. Unfortunately, this agency has viewed alcoholism, not as a primary disease, but as a symptom of psychological inadequacy. In the name of preventive education, for example, NIAAA widely disseminated in the schools and in other community organizations the idea that irresponsible drinking causes alcoholism and that alcoholism can be prevented by learning to drink responsibly. Consistent with this philosophy, NIAAA turned over the accreditation of all alcoholism programs to a panel of psychiatrists in the Joint Commission on Accreditation of Hospitals (JCAH).

The issue that the federal government in general and NIAAA in particular must address is this: Is alcoholism a physiological disease, or is it a symptom of psychological and social problems? As long as NIAAA continues to give credence to the mental health view of alcoholism, the agency will remain one of the major obstacles to public and professional acceptance of the substantial body of research that firmly establishes alcoholism as a primary, physiological disease.

The Individual

Alcoholics and their families cannot afford to wait for physicians to be educated, federal government programs to be realigned, treatment programs to be modified, and laws to be changed. Rather than wait in the hope that someone or something else will protect them, they should instead take responsibility and protect themselves. Having read this book, they will be armed with the basic facts about the disease. They will know that alcoholics are not morally or psychologically defective people, but innocent victims of a chronic and progressive disease. They will know the warning signs of alcoholism, and they will know how to get into treatment. All who understand the disease can join forces to enlighten others. They can insist on change in all areas of community involvement, including the health and social agencies, the judiciary system, and federal, state, and local programs.

Each person's role in the movement toward a complete and unprejudiced understanding of alcoholism may seem small and insignificant. And yet individuals can truly move mountains. Society is not a solid block with one mind and heart, but a changing and shifting collection of millions of different people. When enough people change and devote their energies to eliminating the myths and misconceptions surrounding alcoholism, they will be able to build on the new understanding and create a new era of enlightenment for the alcoholic, those who love him, and all the rest of us whose lives are affected by his disease.

Notes and References

CHAPTER 1

Epigraph. From "Drunkenness a Vice, Not a Disease," a
    paper by J. E. Todd, read at the General Association at
    Middletown, Conn., June 21, 1882, and by vote of that
    body printed and distributed to the churches. (Quoted in
    E. M. Jellinek, *The Disease Concept of Alcoholism*,
    [New Haven, Conn.:Hillhouse Press, 1960], p. 139.)
1. The symposium on "Research Priorities on Alcohol" was
    sponsored by the Rutgers Center of Alcohol Studies and
    Rutgers University from October 7-9, 1977. The proceed-
    ings of this symposium are contained in *The Journal of
    Studies on Alcohol*, Suppl. no. 8, November 1979, Mark
    Keller, special editor.
2. The Devine, Gross, Chafetz, and Anderson quotations
    were reported in *The Alcoholism Report*, January 25,
    1974; July 12, 1974; January 11, 1974; and December 14,
    1974, respectively. The Dornan quotation was reported in
    The Congressional Record, vol. 125, no. 147, October 25,
    1979.
3. *Human Behavior*, vol. 1, no. 1 (Jan./Feb. 1972), p. 39.
4. *The General Mills American Family Report: Family Health
    in an Era of Stress*, conducted by Yankelovich, Skelly
    and White, Inc. (available from General Mills, Inc., 9200
    Wayzata Boulevard, Minneapolis, Minnesota 55440).
5. These statistics are gleaned from various estimates by
    authorities in the field of alcoholism. The National Insti-
    tute on Alcohol Abuse and Alcoholism (NIAAA) *4th Re-
    port to Congress on Alcohol and Health*, released January
    19, 1981, is the source of many of these figures; *The Alco-
    holism Report*, "the authoritative newsletter for professionals

in the field of alcoholism," is another valuable source of information and facts about alcoholism. *The Alcoholism Report* is published 24 times a year by JSL Reports. For subscription information, contact JSL Reports, 1264 National Press Building, Washington, D.C. 20045.

CHAPTER 2

Epigraph. Chauncey D. Leake, professor of medicine at Ohio State University, at a symposium called "Alcoholism," sponsored by the American Association for the Advancement of Science, 1957.

1. The two classic reference texts on alcohol and alcoholism attest to alcohol's stimulating properties at low doses. In the conclusion to *Actions of Alcohol* (Amsterdam: Elsevier Publishing Co., 1970), authors H. Wallgren and H. Barry say: "Most studies of nerve conduction and transmission, EEG records, and behavioral performance indicate stimulant actions of low doses and depressant actions of high doses" (vol. 2, p. 797). In "Effects of Alcohol on the Neuron," in *The Biology of Alcoholism*, ed. B. Kissin and H. Begleiter (New York: Plenum Press, 1972), R.G. Grenell summarizes: "Neuronal activity is stimulated by low concentrations and depressed by high concentrations of alcohol" (vol. 2, p. 17).

2. The World Health Organization published its definitions in *Alcohol and Alcoholism—Report of an Expert Committee (Geneva, 1955), Technical Report 94.*

3. Berton Roueché, *The Neutral Spirit: A Portrait of Alcohol* (Boston: Little, Brown, and Co., 1960), p. 62.

CHAPTER 3

1. Lieber summarized his research in an article titled, "The Metabolism of Alcohol," in the March 1976 issue of *Scientific American*, pp.25-33. In this article, Lieber suggests that increased microsomal ethanol oxidizing activity (MEOS) in alcoholics is a possible factor in high acetaldehyde levels. Intensified MEOS activity would result in faster metabolism of alcohol to acetaldehyde. For

a detailed review of Lieber's research on acetaldehyde
levels in alcoholics, and nonalcoholics, see C.S. Lieber, Y.
Hasumara, R. Teschke, S. Matsuzaki, and M. Korsten,
"The Effect of Chronic Ethanol Consumption on Acetaldehyde Metabolism," in *The Role of Acetaldehyde in the
Actions of Ethanol*, ed. K.O. Lindros and C.J.P. Ericksson
(Helsinki: Finnish Foundation for Alcohol Studies, vol.
23, 1975), pp. 83-104.

2. Marc A. Schuckit and V. Rayses, "Ethanol Ingestion:
Differences in Blood Acetaldehyde Concentrations in Relatives of Alcoholics and Controls," *Science*, vol. 203 (1979),
p. 54.

3. Lieber speculated in the *Scientific American* (see n. 1
above) that the high acetaldehyde level may be responsible for altering the mitochondria. He summarized: "The
alcoholic may therefore be the victim of a vicious circle: a
high acetaldehyde level impairs mitochondrial function in
the liver, acetaldehyde metabolism is decreased, more
acetaldehyde accumulates and causes further liver damage"
(p. 32).

4. Marc Schuckit, "Alcoholism and Genetics: Possible Biological Mediators," in *Biological Psychiatry*, vol. 15 (1980),
no. 3, pp. 437-47.

5. Brain amines (or neurotransmitters) are responsible for
relaying information from one neuron to another. Each of
the 30 different substances known or suspected to be
transmitters in the brain (including serotonin, norepinephrine, and dopamine) has a characteristic excitatory or
inhibitory effect on neurons. See *Scientific American*,
September 1979, pp. 134-49, for more information on the
actions of these complex chemical substances.

6. The theory that acetaldehyde, rather than or in addition
to alcohol itself, may be responsible for addiction is
gaining popularity among researchers. Acetaldehyde's specific actions in the brain have not yet been pinpointed,
but several researchers have made intriguing proposals.
See V.E. Davis and M.J. Walsh, "Alcohol, Amines, Alkaloids:
A Possible Biochemical Basis for Alcohol Addiction," *Science*,
vol. 167 (1970), pp. 1005-7; and G. Cohen and M.A.
Collins, "Alkaloids from Catecholamines in Adrenal Tissue:

Possible Role in Alcoholism," *Science,* vol. 167 (1970), pp. 1749-51.

7. R.D. Myers and W.L. Veale, "Alcohol Preference in the Rat: Reduction Following Depletion of Brain Serotonin," *Science,* vol. 160 (1968), pp. 1469-71.

8. L. Ahtee and K. Eriksson, "5-Hydroxytryptamine and 5-hydroxyindoleacetic acid content in brain of rat strains selected for their alcohol intake," *Physiology and Behavior,* vol. 8 (1972), pp. 123-26; and J.L. Perhach, Jr., R.H. Cox, Jr., and H.C. Ferguson, "Possible Role of Serotonin in the Voluntary Selection of Ethanol by Mice," *Proceedings of the Federation of American Societies for Experimental Biology,* vol. 32 (1973), p. 697.

9. R.D. Myers and C.L. Melchior, "Alcohol Drinking: Abnormal Intake Caused by Tetrahydropapaveroline in Brain," *Science,* vol. 196 (1977), pp. 554-56.

10. Donald Goodwin, *Is Alcoholism Hereditary?* (New York: Oxford University Press, 1976).

11. *Ibid.,* p. 77.

12. B. Kissin and H. Begleiter, eds., *The Biology of Alcoholism* (New York: Plenum Press, 1974), vol. 3, p. 10.

13. In June 1980, Harvard Medical School received a $5.8 million gift from Joseph E. Seagram and Sons, Inc., U.S. subsidiary of the world's largest distiller and winemaker. The gift is to be used for research on the fundamental biological, chemical, and genetic aspects of alcohol metabolism and alcoholism. Dr. Bert Vallee is directing the research supported by the grant. From the *Harvard Gazette,* June 27, 1980.

14. D. Fenna, L. Mix, O. Schaefer, and J.A.L. Gilbert, "Ethanol Metabolism in Various Racial Groups," *Canadian Medical Association Journal,* vol. 105 (1971), pp. 472-75; and P.H. Wolff, "Ethnic Differences in Alcohol Sensitivity," *Science,* vol. 175 (1972), pp. 449-50.

15. Several sources report higher acetaldehyde levels in Orientals than in Caucasians. See M.A. Korsten, S. Matsuzaki, L. Feinman, and C.S. Lieber, "High Blood Acetaldehyde Levels after Ethanol Administration: Differences between Alcoholic and Nonalcoholic Subjects," *New England Journal of Medicine,* vol. 292 (1975), pp. 386-89, J.A. Ewing, B.A. Rouse, and E.D. Pellezzari, "Alcohol Sensitivity and

Ethnic Background," *American Journal of Psychiatry*, vol. 131 (1974), pp. 206-10; and T.E. Reed, H. Kalant, R.J. Gibbins, B.M. Kapur, and J.G. Rankin, "Alcohol and Acetaldehyde Metabolism in Caucasians, Chinese and Amerinds," *Canadian Medical Association Journal*, vol. 115 (1976), pp. 851-55.

16. James R. Milam, *The Emergent Comprehensive Concept of Alcoholism* (ACA Press, P.O. Box 286, Kirkland, WA 98033).

CHAPTER 4

1. C.S. Lieber, and L.M. Dicarli, "The Role of the Hepatic Microsomal Ethanol Oxidizing System (MEOS) for Ethanol Metabolism in Vivo," *Journal of Pharmacology and Experimental Therapeutics*, vol. 181 (1972), pp. 279-87.

2. J.H. Chin and D.B. Goldstein, "Drug Tolerance in Biomembranes: A Spin Label Study of the Effects of Ethanol," *Science*, vol. 196 (1977), pp. 684-85.

3. H. Wallgren and H. Barry, *Actions of Alcohol* (Amsterdam: Elsevier Publishing Co., 1970), vol. 2, p. 496.

4. Numerous studies attest to alcohol's ability to improve the performance of alcoholics in a variety of mental and motor skills; see, for example, Wallgren and Barry, *op. cit.*, pp. 479-618 (chapter 9). In another work, Jack Mendelson and Nancy Mello comment on the wide differences in functioning between alcoholics and nonalcoholics: "Most social drinkers will show significant signs of intoxication at blood levels between 100 and 150 mg/100 ml and will be grossly intoxicated at levels above 200 mg/100 ml. Stupor and coma may occur at levels above 300 mg/ml. Alcohol addicts who have adequate liver function and who have developed a high degree of tolerance will not show such impairments. For example, alcohol addicts with blood ethanol levels between 200 and 300 mg/100 ml can perform quite accurately in tasks requiring psychomotor skills and good cognitive and memory function" (J.H. Mendelson and N.K. Mello, eds., *The Diagnosis and Treatment of Alcoholism* [New York: McGraw-Hill, 1979], p. 11).

5. For a general review of alcohol's "normalizing" effect on autonomic nervous system functions, see B. Kissin, J. Schenker, and A. Schenker, "The Acute Effects of Ethyl Alcohol and Chlorpromazine on Certain Physiological Functions in Alcoholics," *Quarterly Journal of Studies on Alcohol,* vol. 20 (1959), pp. 480-92.

CHAPTER 5

1. Marty Mann, *Marty Mann Answers Your Questions about Drinking and Alcoholism* (rev. ed.; New York: Holt, Rinehart and Winston, 1981), p. 52.
2. Benjamin Karpman, *The Hangover: A Critical Study in the Psycho-dynamics of Alcoholism* (Springfield, Ill., 1957); quoted in Berton Roueché, *The Neutral Spirit: A Portrait of Alcohol* (Boston: Little, Brown, and Co., 1960), pp. 129-30.
3. Benjamin Kissin, "Biological Investigations in Alcohol Research," *Journal of Studies on Alcohol,* Suppl. no. 8 ("Research Priorities on Alcohol"), November 1979, Mark Keller, special editor, pp. 172-73.
4. *Ibid.,* p. 171
5. B. Kissin, M.M. Gross, and I. Schutz, "Correlation of Urinary Biogenic Amines with Sleep Stages in Chronic Alcoholization and Withdrawal," in *Alcohol Intoxication and Withdrawal: Experimental Studies* (New York: Plenum Press, 1973), ed. M.M. Gross ("Advances in Experimental Medicine and Biology," vol. 35), vol. 1, pp. 281-89.
6. One research team reported sleep disturbances in alcoholics abstinent for as long as 4 years. See A.M.I. Wagman and R.P. Allen, "Effects of Alcohol Ingestion and Abstinence on Slow Wave Sleep of Alcoholics," in *ibid.,* pp. 453-66.
7. Clinical experience, Alcenas Hospital, Kirkland, WA, one of the few treatment centers in the country which stress comprehensive nutritional therapy during and after treatment.
8. E.M. Jellinek, *The Disease Concept of Alcoholism* (New Haven, Conn.: Hillhouse Press, 1960), p. 139.

CHAPTER 6

1. W. Schmidt and R.E. Popham, unpublished data, printed in Yedy Israel's paper, "Researching the Biology of Alcoholism: One Way of Seeing It," in the *Journal of Studies on Alcohol*, Suppl. no. 8, November 1979, Mark Keller, special editor, p. 184.
2. Lawrence Feinman and Charles S. Lieber comment on the relationship between fatty liver, hepatitis, and cirrhosis in their article, "Liver Disease in Alcoholism," in *The Biology of Alcoholism*, ed. B. Kissin and H. Begleiter (New York: Plenum Press, 1972): ". . . fatty liver and alcoholic hepatitis . . . usually precede cirrhosis by many years and often eventually co-exist with it. However, there is no conclusive evidence that these latter lesions are necessary for cirrhosis to develop" (vol. 3, p. 321).
3. James R. Hoon, M.D., "Hair of the Dog: A Gastrocamera Study," in the *Journal of the American Medical Association*, vol. 229 (1974), no. 2, pp. 184-85.
4. W. Schmidt and J. DeLint, "Mortality Experiences of Male and Female Alcoholics," vol. 30 (1969), pp. 112-18.
5. Benjamin Kissin and Maureen M. Kaley, "Alcohol and Cancer," in *The Biology of Alcoholism*, ed. Kissin and Begleiter, vol. 3, p. 481.

CHAPTER 8

Epigraph. This statement was made by Thomas Fleming, M.D., Medical Director of Little Hill–Alina Lodge, New Jersey, in a panel discussion which was organized by the magazine *Patient Care* and reprinted in their February 28, 1979, issue.

1. Vernon E. Johnson, *I'll Quit Tomorrow* (New York: Harper & Row, Publishers, 1973).
2. The National Council of Alcoholism publishes numerous pamphlets of interest to both laymen and professionals. Its stated purpose is to work for the prevention and control of alcoholism through programs of public and professional education, community services, and the pro-

motion of alcoholism research. Write to the Council at 733 Third Avenue, New York, N.Y., 10017.

Comprehensive Care Corporation operates the largest chain of private alcoholism treatment programs in the United States. For information, write CompCare Publications, 2415 Annapolis Lane, Suite 140, Minneapolis, Minn. 55441.

3. From an interview with Wilbur Mills in *Overview,* the journal of Overlook Hospital in Summit, N.J., vol. 1, no. 3 (Fall 1980).

CHAPTER 9

1. Thomas Trotter, "An Essay, Medical, Philosophical, and Chemical, on Drunkenness and Its Effects on the Human Body."
2. *Twelve Steps and Twelve Traditions,* p. 74. Both *Alcoholics Anonymous* (3rd ed., 1976) and *Twelve Steps and Twelve Traditions* (1952) are published by A.A. World Services, New York, N.Y. 10017.
3. From *Twelve Steps and Twelve traditions*.
4. H. Wallgren and H. Barry, *Actions of Alcohol* (Amsterdam: Elsevier Publishing Co., 1970), vol. 1, p. 5.
5. Alcenas Hospital was cofounded by James Milam and Dorris Hutchison in Kirkland, Washington, in 1970. In April 1981 the hospital was purchased by Comprehensive Care Corporation.
6. Father Martin made this comment in his widely acclaimed film "Chalktalk." Father Martin is a lively and unflagging crusader in alcoholism education. "Chalktalk," a film of a speech he gave to military personnel, is a classic example of Father Martin at his best—impassioned, excitable, and brutally frank—and is highly recommended for use in education and treatment programs.

CHAPTER 10

Epigraph: From *The Tranquilizing of America,* by Richard Hughes and Robert Brewin (New York: Warner Books, Inc., 1979), p. 41.

1. Charles Lieber's research on drug and alcohol interactions is summarized in the March 1976 issue of *Scientific American*.

2. *The Biology of Alcoholism*, ed. B. Kissin and H. Begleiter (New York: Plenum Press, 1972), vol. 3, p. 112.

3. Benjamin Kissin discusses the concept of reactivation of physical dependence in his article "Biological Investigations in Alcohol Research," *Journal of Studies on Alcohol*, suppl. no. 8 ("Research Priorities on Alcohol"), November 1979, Mark Keller, special editor, pp. 170-71.

4. Betty Ford, with Chris Chase, *The Times of My Life* (New York: Ballantine Books, 1979), p. 307.

5. *Ibid.*, pp. 310-11.

6. *The Tranquilizing of America*, p. 77.

7. *Ibid.*, pp. 36-37.

8. *Patient Care*, February 28, 1979, p. 45.

9. *Physicians Desk Reference* (Oradell, N.J.: Economic Book Division, 1980), p. 591.

10. Joe Kwentus and Leslie F. Major, "Disulfiram in the Treatment of Alcoholism," *Journal of Studies on Alcohol*, vol. 40, no. 5 (May 1979), pp. 428-46.

11. S.C. Liddon and R. Satran, "Disulfiram (Antabuse) Psychosis," *American Journal of Psychiatry*, vol. 123 (1967), pp. 1284-89; and N.H. Rathod, "Toxic Effects of Disulfiram Therapy; with Two Case Reports," *Quarterly Journal of Studies on Alcohol*, vol. 19 (1958), pp. 418-27.

12. A.H. Nora, J.J. Nora, and J. Blu, "Limb-Reduction Anomalies in Infants born to Disulfiram-treated Alcoholic Mothers," *Lancet*, Vol. 2 (1977), p. 664.

13. For a review of various articles on the subject of the interaction of Antabuse with other medications, see article by Kwentus and Major cited in n. 10 above, pp. 434-35.

14. John M. Rainey, Jr., "Disulfiram Toxicity and Carbon Disulfide Poisoning," *American Journal of Psychiatry*, vol. 134, no. 4 (April 1, 1977).

15. Ralph E. Vodarken, "Ethylene Dibromide and Disulfiram: A Lethal Combination," *Journal of the American Medical Association*, vol. 239 (June 1978), p. 2783.

CHAPTER 11

1. Ira Cisin, discussion, *Journal of Studies on Alcohol*, suppl. no. 8 ("Research Priorities on Alcohol"), November 1979, Mark Keller, special editor, p. 52.

2. David J. Armor, J. Michael Polich, Harriet B. Stambul, *Alcoholism and Treatment* (New York: John Wiley & Sons, 1978). On page 99, the authors describe the "normal" drinking criteria: ". . . the recovered alcoholic who is classified as a normal drinker must meet *all* of the following criteria:

    1. Daily comsumption of less than 3 ounces of ethanol.
    2. Typical quantities on drinking days less than 5 ounces.
    3. No tremors reported.
    4. No serious symptoms."

    Serious symptoms were then classified as "frequent episodes of three or more of the following: blackouts, missing work, morning drinking, missing meals, and being drunk. 'Frequent' means three or more episodes of blackouts or missing work in the past month, or five or more episodes of the other symptoms."

3. *Alcoholism Report* (Washington, D.C.: JSL Reports), October 17, 1972.

4. *Alcoholism Report* August 25, 1978.

5. *Alcoholism Report* January 11, 1980.

6. Eaton's comment: *Alcoholism Report*, September 24, 1973 (special issue); Bourne: *Alcoholism Report*, December 23, 1977; Brock: *Alcoholism Report*, January 27, 1978; and Ohlms: *Alcoholism Report*, July 27, 1979.

7. M. Hayman, "Current Attitudes to Alcoholism of Psychiatrists in Southern California," *American Journal of Psychiatry*, vol. 112 (1956), pp. 484-93.

Suggested Reading List

REFERENCES

Actions of Alcohol, by Henrik Wallgren and Herbert Barry III. New York: Elsevier Publishing Co., Inc. 1970.
Volume 1: Biochemical, Physiological, and Psychological Aspects
Volume 2: Chronic and Clinical Aspects
A comprehensive review of experimental work on alcohol and its effects on animals and humans.

The Biology of Alcoholism, edited by Benjamin Kissin and Henri Begleiter. New York: Plenum Press.
Volume 1: Biochemistry (1971)
Volume 2: Physiology and Behavior (1972)
Volume 3: Clinical Pathology (1974)
Volume 4: Social Aspects of Alcoholism (1976)
Volume 5: Treatment and Rehabilitation of the Chronic Alcoholic (1977)
A thorough examination of the current knowledge of biological mechanisms involved in the development of alcoholism.

GENERAL WORKS

The Disease Concept of Alcoholism, by E.M. Jellinek. New Haven, Conn.: Hillhouse Press, 1960.
The "classic" work by one of the great pioneers in alcoholism theory and treatment which catapulted the theory that alcoholism is a disease into public awareness.

I'll Quit Tomorrow, by Vernon E. Johnson. New York: Harper and Row, 1973.
    The best parts of this informative and readable book are the chapters detailing the symptoms of alcoholism, particularly rationalizations and denials, and the chapters on intervention strategies and techniques.

Marty Mann Answers Your Questions about Drinking and Alcoholism, by Marty Mann. Rev. ed. New York: Holt, Rinehart & Winston, 1981.
    One of the first women members of Alcoholics Anonymous, and the founder of the National Council on Alcoholism, answers the most frequently asked questions about drinking and alcoholism.

The Neutral Spirit: A Portrait of Alcohol, by Berton Roueché. Boston: Little, Brown & Co., 1960.
    A lively, illuminating review of alcohol and its use from ancient to modern man.

Primer on Alcoholism, by Marty Mann. New York: Rinehart & Co., Inc., 1950.
    An overview for both the alcoholic and the nonalcoholic of how people drink, how to recognize alcoholics, and what to do about them. Revised and updated in 1958 as *New Primer on Alcoholism.*

ALCOHOLICS ANONYMOUS

A.A. literature is not available through bookstores but can be purchased through local A.A. offices or ordered from General Services Board of A.A., 468 Park Avenue South, New York, N.Y. 10016.

A.A. Comes of Age. A brief history of A.A. by Bill Wilson, cofounder of A.A. New York, 1957.

Alcoholics Anonymous. 1976 ed. The "Bible" of A.A. literature, this book outlines the basic A.A. program and includes 44 personal histories of individuals who found recovery from alcoholism through A.A.

Twelve Steps and Twelve Traditions. Referred to in A.A. as the "12 by 12," this book elaborates the basic guidelines of the A.A. program.

DRUGS

I'm Dancing as Fast as I Can, by Barbara Gordon. New York: Harper and Row, 1979.

One woman's personal account of her addiction to Valium, her agonizing cold-turkey withdrawal, and her battle to get well again. A powerful indictment of the mental health system and the attitude that the fault for addiction to prescribed drugs lies in the individual.

The New Handbook of Prescription Drugs, by Richard Burack, M.D., and Dr. Fred J. Fox. New York: Ballantine, rev. ed. 1975.

This handy reference book provides basic information on drugs, generic and brand price comparisons, and an illuminating look at the drug industry's control over the flow of information to the medical profession.

The Times of My Life, by Betty Ford with Chris Chase. New York: Ballantine Books, 1979.

Chapters 38 and 39 of this special edition of the former first lady's biography tell of her addiction to alcohol and pills, her family's intervention, her recovery, and her commitment to live "this beautiful new life of mine to the fullest."

The Tranquilizing of America, by Richard Hughes and Robert Brewin. New York: Warner Books, 1979.

A hard-hitting, informative, and highly readable look at prescription drug use in the United States.

HEREDITY

Is Alcoholism Hereditary? by Donald Goodwin, M.D. New York: Oxford University Press, 1976.

The author is a journalist as well as a physician and researcher, and he writes with clarity about the role of heredity in determining alcoholism. The discussion about his adoption studies conducted in Denmark is particularly informative.

NUTRITION

Alcoholism: The Nutritional Approach, by Roger J. Williams. Austin: University of Texas Press, 1959.

A pioneer in the field of alcoholism and nutrition presents his genetrophic concept that alcoholism develops from a genetically determined nutritional disorder in this short, easy-to-read book.

Nutrigenetics, by Dr. R.O. Brennan with William C. Mulligan. Foreword by Roger J. Williams. New York: M. Evans & Co., Inc. 1975.

This fascinating and easy-to-read book presents the theory that combined genetic (hereditary) and nutritional (food/nourishment) deficiencies may cause hypoglycemia. Also included are the caloric and nutritional values of common foods and menus and snack suggestions.

Nutrition against Disease, by Roger J. Williams. New York: Pitman, 1971.

A guide to the prevention or control of disease through improved nutrition.

PERSONAL ACCOUNTS

Bill W., by Robert Thomsen. New York: Popular Library, 1975.

A biography of Bill Wilson, cofounder of Alcoholics Anonymous.

Off the Sauce, by Lewis Meyer. New York: Collier Books, 1967.

An anecdotal account by a man who finally made it "off the sauce" with the help of A.A.

Prodigal Shepherd, by Father Ralph Pfau and Al Hirshberg. New York: Popular Library, 1958.

A priest's account of his addiction to drink and the courage he ultimately found to help himself and others.

A Sensitive, Passionate Man, by Barbara Mahoney. New York: David McKay Co., 1974.

The slow, agonizing destruction of a life and a family by alcoholism has never been more graphically described than in this true-to-life account.

Appendix A

Medications Containing Alcohol Commonly Stocked in
Most Hospitals and Pharmacies

Drug	Percentage of Alcohol	Drug	Percentage of Alcohol
Actol Expectorant Syrup	12.5	Dimacol Liquid	4.75
Alertonic	0.45	Donnatal Elixir	23.0
Alurate Elixir	20.0	Donnagel Suspension	3.8
Ambenyl Expectorant	5.0	Donnagel PG Suspension	5.0
Anahist	0.5	Dramamine Liquid	5.0
Aromatic Elixir	22.0	Feosol Elixir	5.0
Anaspaz—Pb Liquid	15.0	Fer—In—Sol Syrup	5.0
Asbron Elixir	15.0	Theolixir (Elixir Theophylline)	20.0
Atarax Syrup	0.5	Elixophy	20.0
Bactrim Suspension	0.3	Elixophylline—K1	10.0
Tr. Belladonna	67.0	Ephedrine Sulfate Syrup U.S.P.	3.0
Benadryl Elixir	14.0	Ephedrine Sulfate Syrup—	
Bentyl—Pb Syrup	19.0	Note U.S.P.	12.0
Benylin Expectorant	5.0	Fer—In—Sol Drops	0.2
Brondecon Elixir	20.0	Geriplex—FS	18.0
Bronkelixir	19.0	Gevrabon Liquid	18.0
Butibel Elixir	7.0	Kaon Elixir	5.0
Calcidrine Syrup	6.0	Kaochlor	3.8
Cas Evac	18.0	Iberet Liquid	1.0
Aromatic Cascara Sagroda	18.0	Isuprel Comp. Elixir	19.0
Carbrital Elixir	18.0	Syrup Ipecac	2.0
Cerose & Cerose DM		Hydryllin Comp.	5.0
Expectorant	2.5	Hycotuss Expectorant & Syrup	10.0
Cheracol & Cheracol D.	3.0	Kay—Ciel Elixir	4.0
Choledyl Elixir	20.0	Lanoxin Elixir Pediatric	10.0
Chlor—Trimeton Syrup	7.0	Liquid Lomotil	15.0
Cologel Liquid	5.0	Luffyllin—GG Elixir	17.0
Citra Forte Syrup	2.0	Marax Syrup	5.0
Coldene Cough Syrup	15.0	Mediatric Liquid	15.0
Conar Expectorant	5.0	Modane Liquid	5.0
Coryban D	7.5	Mellaril Concentrate	3.0
Cosanyl DM & Cosanyl Syrup	6.0	Mesopin Elixir	12.5
Copavin Cmpd Elixir	7.0	Minocin Syrup	5.0
Darvon—N Suspension	1.0	Nembutal Elixir	18.0
Decadron Elixir	5.0	Novahistine DH	5.0
Dexedrine Elixir	10.0	Nicol Elixir	10.0
Demazin Syrup	7.5	Novahistine Expectorant	5.0
Dilaudid Cough Syrup	5.0	Novahistine Elixir	5.0
Elixir Dimetane	3.0	Novahistine DMX	10.0
Dimetane Expectorant	3.5	Nico—Metrazol Elixir	15.0
Dimetane Expectorant—D.C.	3.5	Nyquil Cough Syrup	25.0
Doxinate Liquid	5.0	Mol Iron Liquid	4.75
Dimetapp Elixir	2.3	Organidin Elixir	23.75

Drug	Percentage of Alcohol
Ornacol Liquid	8.0
Tincture Paregoric	45.0
Parapectolin	0.69
Parelixir	18.0
Periactin Syrup	5.0
Pertussin 8 Hour Syrup	9.5
Phenergan Expectorant Plain	7.0
Phenobarbital Elixir	14.0
Phenergan Expectorant with Codeine	7.0
Phenergan Expectorant V.C., Plain	7.0
Phenergan Expectorant V.C., with Codeine	7.0
Phenergan Expectorant Pediatric	7.0
Phenergan Syrup Fortis (25mg)	1.5
Polaramine Expectorant	7.2
P.B.Z. Expectorant with Ephedrine	6.0
Propadrine Elixir HCl	16.0
P.B.Z. Expectorant with Codeine and Ephedrine	6.0
Quibron Elixir	15.0
Robitussin Syrup	3.5
Robitussin A.C. Syrup	3.5
Robitussin PE	1.4
Robitussin D.M. and Robitussin C.F.	1.4
Rondec D.M. Syrup and Drops	0.6
Roniacol Elixir	8.6
Serpasil Elixir	12.0
Tedral Elixir	15.0
Temaril Syrup	5.7
Terpin Hydrate Elixir	42.0
Terpin Hydrate Elixir with Codeine	42.0
Theo Organidin Elixir	15.0
Triaminic Expectorant	5.0
Triaminic Expectorant D.H.	5.0
Tussend Liquid	5.0
Tussar—2 Syrup	5.0
Tussi—Organidin Expectorant	15.0
Tussar S.F. Syrup	12.0
Tuss—Ornade Syrup	7.5
Tylenol Elixir	7.0
Tylenol with Codeine Elixir	7.0
Tylenol Drops	7.0
Ulo—Syrup	6.65

Drug	Percentage of Alcohol
Valadol Liquid	9.0
Valpin—PB Elixir & Valpin	5.3
Vita Metrazol Elixir	15.0
Vicks Formula 44	10.0
Potassium Chloride Sol. (Standard)	10.0

(a no alcohol solution can be requested)

NOTE:

1. Mouthwashes—Scope, Listerine, Cepacol, Colgate 100, Micrin all have approximately 15-25%.
2. All elixirs contain some alcohol.
3. The following anti-tussives do *not* contain alcohol:
   *Hycodan Syrup
   *Hycomine Syrup
   Triaminicol Syrup
   *Tussionex Suspension
   Orthoxicol Syrup
   Actified C Expectorant
   Omnituss
   Ipsatol Syrup
4. Other non-alcoholic liquids:
   Chloraseptic mouthwash/gargle
   Liquiprin (acetaminophen)
   Dilantin Suspension
   Alupent Syrup
   *Noctec Syrup
   *Vistaril Suspension
   Antacids
   Kaopectate and Parget, etc.
   Sudafed Syrup
   *Quadrinal Suspension
   Actifed Syrup
   Triaminic Syrup
   Naldecon Syrup
   Nydrazid Syrup

*Ingestive medications may contain other addictive substances which may be considered.

Courtesy of
Alcenas Hospital
10322 N.E. 132nd
Kirkland, Washington 98033

Appendix B

GUIDELINES FOR A HYPOGLYCEMIC DIET

The object of this hypoglycemic diet is to eliminate refined carbohydrates and achieve a balance of proteins, natural carbohydrates, and low fat.

The hypoglycemic diet includes three meals a day with three snacks—midmorning, midafternoon, and before bedtime.

Foods are prepared without sugar, white flour, or other refined carbohydrates.

Labels on canned or prepared food should be read to avoid use of sugar, syrups, or honey. Additives and preservatives are implicated in some food intolerances and should be avoided as much as possible.

Foods To Strictly Avoid
Alcoholic beverages of any kind.

Sugar, honey, molasses—includes ice cream, any canned goods (fruits and vegetables) with added sugars, ketchup and other condiments with sugar added.

Soft drinks and fruit-flavored drinks which contain caffeine or added sugars.

Coffee or strong tea, both of which cause a rise, then fall, in blood sugar level.

Medications containing caffeine, such as Anacin, Caffergot, Coricidin, Empirin Compound. All over-the-counter cold and cough medicines need to be checked for alcohol or caffeine content.

Foods to Eat Occasionally or in Moderation
Dried Fruits—raisins, dates, prunes, etc.

Processed meats such as bacon, sausage, or ham.

Breads or cereal products not made with whole grain. White noodles and starches can be replaced by whole grain unprocessed foods. Avoid white flour whenever possible.

Allowable Foods

Most unprocessed, natural foods.

Fresh meats, fish, and fowl.

Dairy products, including milk, plain yogurt, cheeses.

Nuts and seeds (avoid added salt).

Nut butters (without sugar).

Whole grain foods and unprocessed grain products.

All fresh vegetables and fruits and unprocessed juices. Eat or drink them daily.

Artificially sweetened foods or drinks such as diet soda.

Decaffeinated coffee, herbal teas.

Naturally based vitamin and mineral preparations, ideally as prescribed by a knowledgeable physician.

Appendix C

SAMPLE HYPOGLYCEMIC DIET

Breakfast, lunch, and dinner

MONDAY	TUESDAY	WEDNESDAY	THURSDAY
Toast (1) Pork patty (1) Eggs (1) choice Juice, 4 oz. or ½ grapefruit Margarine (1) Jelly Hot or cold cereal ½ cup Coffee, tea, milk*	Whole wheat muffin (1) Bacon (2) Eggs (1) choice Juice, 4 oz. or ½ grapefruit Margarine (1) Jelly Cold cereal Coffee, tea, milk	Whole wheat pancakes (2) or toast (1) Links (2) Eggs (1) choice Juice, 4 oz. or ½ grapefruit Margarine (1) Syrup (1) or jelly Oatmeal ½ cup Coffee, tea, milk	Toast (1) Bacon (2) Eggs (1) choice Juice, 4 oz. or ½ grapefruit Margarine (1) Jelly Hot or cold cereal ½ cup Coffee, tea, milk
Spaghetti ½ cup Meat sauce 4 oz. Italian vegetables ½ cup Garlic wholewheat bread Salad bar w/fruit bowl Coffee, tea, milk	Baked snapper 3 oz. Tartar sauce Lemon wedge French beans w/red peppers ½ cup Peanut butter cookies (2) Salad bar w/cole slaw Coffee, tea, milk	Hamburgers Wholewheat bun Trimmings Baked beans ½ cup Salad bar w/fruit Coffee, tea, milk	Beef vegetable soup 7 oz. Reuben sandwich on rye bread Salad bar w/lime fruit mold Coffee, tea, milk
Orange glazed brisket 3 oz. Broccoli ½ cup Beets ½ cup 7 grain roll Margarine Salad bar Coffee, tea, milk	Tahitian chicken 3 oz. Brown rice ½ cup Oriental vegetables ½ cup Wholewheat bread (1) Margarine Salad bar Coffee, tea, milk	Corned beef 3 oz. Boiled red potato ½ cup Cabbage ½ cup Rye roll Margarine Salad bar w/fruit Coffee, tea, milk	Pot roast 3 oz. Gravy 1 oz. Mashed potatoes ½ cup Pineapple carrots ½ cup 7 grain roll Margarine Macaroni salad ½ cup Salad bar Coffee, tea, milk

*Coffee is decaffeinated. Teas are herbal.

FRIDAY	SATURDAY	SUNDAY
Whole wheat blueberry muffin (1) or toast (1) Pork patty (1) Eggs (1) choice Juice, 4 oz., or ½ grapefruit Margarine (1) Jelly Cold cereal Coffee, tea, milk	Whole wheat pancakes (2) or toast (1) Links (2) Eggs (1) choice Juice, 4 oz. or ½ grapefruit Margarine (1) Syrup (1) or Jelly Hot or cold cereal Coffe, tea, milk	Toast (1) Bacon (2) Eggs (1) choice Juice, 4 oz. or ½ grapefruit Margarine (1) Jelly 4 grain cereal or cold cereal Coffee, tea, milk
Tuna noodle casserole Bean medley ½ cup (Garnish w/½ apple) Salad bar w/cole slaw Coffee, tea, milk	Roast veal 3 oz. Lima beans ½ cup Corn ½ cup Wholewheat roll Margarine Salad bar w/fruit bowl Coffee, tea, milk	Roast turkey 3 oz. Dressing ½ cup Gravy 1 oz. Cranberry cup Asparagus ½ cup Salad bar Coffee, tea, milk
Steak 4 oz. Baked potato ½ cup French beans w/almonds ½ cup (Garnish w/½ orange) Salad bar Coffee, tea, milk	Stuffed green pepper 3 oz. W/tomato sauce 1 oz. Scandinavian vegetable ½ cup Potato salad Corn chips Salad bar Coffee, tea, milk	Veal cutlet 3 oz. Italian beans ½ cup (Garnish w/orange ½) Salad bar Coffee, tea, milk

SAMPLE SNACKS

Midmorning, afternoon and evening

MONDAY	TUESDAY	WEDNESDAY	THURSDAY
Strawberry yogurt shake 6 oz. Coffee, herb tea	Pineapple yogurt shake 6 oz. Coffee, herb tea	Banana yogurt shake 6 oz. Coffee, herb tea	Blackberry yogurt shake 6 oz. Coffee, herb tea
Petite banana (1) Sugar free cookie Milk, coffee, herb tea	½ orange Triscuit Milk, coffee, herb tea	½ apple Cracker Milk, coffee, herb tea	Celery sticks w/peanut butter 1 oz. Milk, coffee, herb tea
Roast beef 1 oz. Cheddar cheese 1 oz. Cracker Milk, coffee	Roast pork loin 1 oz. Jack cheese 1 oz. Cracker Milk, coffee	Turkey salad ½ cup Cracker Milk, coffee	Roast veal 1 oz. Swiss cheese 1 oz. Cracker Milk, coffee

FRIDAY	SATURDAY	SUNDAY
Mixed fruit yogurt shake 6 oz. Coffee, herb tea	Blueberry yogurt shake 6 oz. Coffee, herb tea	Spiced apple yogurt shake 6 oz. Coffee, herb tea
Deviled egg (1) Triscuit Milk, coffee, herb tea	Petite banana (1) Cracker Milk, coffee, herb tea	Apple (1) Cracker Milk, coffee, herb tea
Boiled brisket 1 oz. Munster cheese 1 oz. Cracker Milk, coffee	Chicken drumsticks (3) Cracker Milk, coffee	Corned beef 1 oz. Gouda cheese 1 oz. Cracker Milk, coffee

Appendix D

Sample prescription form proposed by the National Clearinghouse for Alcohol Information.

A CHECK-MARK HAS BEEN PLACED IN THE BOX PRECEDING THE CLASS OF DRUG WHICH BEST DESCRIBES THE ONE WHICH I HAVE PRESCRIBED.

CAUTION: The medication I have prescribed for you has been reported to interact with alcoholic beverages. Some of these interactions are particularly dangerous, and I have checked below the class of drug which covers the one I am prescribing.

If you have any questions concerning your medication, do not hesitate to ask me. The pharmacist who fills this prescription can also give you valuable information on alcohol and other drugs, and you may wish to send for the free alcohol and drug information provided by: The National Clearinghouse for Alcohol Information, P.O. Box 2345, Department RX, Rockville, Maryland 20852.

Phone: Dr. J. Smith   Office Hours:
(123) 765-4321 Office   1234 Main Street   Week Days
(123) 123-4567 Home   Dayton, Ohio 09876   9:00 A.M.—3:00 P.M.
                                                        Saturday 11:00—2:00

R̷

☐ ANALGESICS, NARCOTIC
(Demerol, Darvon, Dilaudid, etc.) When used alone, both alcohol and narcotic drugs cause a reduction in the function of the central nervous system. When used together, this effect is even greater, and may lead to loss of effective breathing function (respiratory arrest). Death may occur.

☐ ANALGESICS, NON-NARCOTIC
(Aspirin, APC, Pabalate, etc.) Even when used alone, some non-prescription pain relievers can cause bleeding in the stomach and intestines. Alcohol also irritates the stomach and can aggravate the bleeding, especially in ulcer patients.

☐ ANTIALCOHOL PREPARATIONS
(Antabuse, Calcium Carbamide) Use of alcohol with medications prescribed to help alcoholic patients keep from drinking results in nausea, vomiting, headache, high blood pressure and possible erratic heart beat, and can result in death.

☐ ANTICOAGULANTS
(Panwarfin, Dicumarol, Sintrom, etc.) Alcohol can increase the ability of these drugs to stop blood clotting, which in turn can lead to life-threatening or fatal hemorrhages.

☐ ANTICONVULSANTS
(Dilantin, Diphenyl, EKKO, etc.) Drinking may lessen the ability of this drug to stop convulsions in a person.

☐ ANTIDEPRESSANTS
(Tofranil, Pertofrane, Triavil, etc.)

226

Alcohol may cause an additional reduction in central nervous system functioning and lessen a person's ability to operate normally. Certain antidepressants in combination with red wines like Chianti may cause a high blood pressure crisis.

☐ ANTIDIABETIC AGENTS/HYPO-GLYCEMICS
(Insulin, Diabenese, Orinase, etc.)
Because of the possible severe reactions to combining alcohol and insulin or the oral antidiabetic agents, and because alcohol interacts unpredictably with them, patients taking any of these medications should avoid alcohol.

☐ ANTIHISTAMINES
(most cold remedies, Actifed, Coricidin, etc.)
Taking alcohol with this class of drugs increases their calming effect and a person can feel quite drowsy, making driving and other activities which require alertness more hazardous.

☐ ANTIHYPERTENSIVE AGENTS
(Serpasil, Aldomet, Esidrix, etc.)
Alcohol may increase the blood pressure lowering capability of some of these drugs, causing dizziness when a person gets up. Some agents will also cause a reduction in the function of the central nervous system.

☐ ANTIINFECTIVE AGENTS/ANTIBIOTICS
(Flagyl, Chloromycetin, Seromycin, etc.)
In combination with alcohol, some may cause nausea, vomiting, and headache, and possibly convulsions, especially those taken for urinary tract infections.

☐ CENTRAL NERVOUS SYSTEM STIMULANTS
(most diet pills, Dexedrine, Caffeine, Ritalin, etc.)
Because the stimulant effect of this class of drugs may reverse the depressant effect of the alcohol on the central nervous system, these drugs can give a false sense of security. They do *not* help intoxicated persons gain control of their movements.

☐ DIURETICS
(Diuril, Lasix, Hydromox, etc.)
Combining alcohol with diuretics may cause reduction in blood pressure, possibly resulting in dizziness when a person stands up.

☐ PSYCHOTROPICS
(Tindal, Mellaril, Thorazine, etc.)
Alcohol and the "major tranquilizers" cause additional depression to the central nervous system function, which can result in severe impairment of voluntary movements such as walking or using the hands. The combination can also cause a loss of effective breathing function and can be fatal.

☐ SEDATIVE HYPNOTICS
(Doriden, Quaalude, Nembutal, etc.)
Alcohol in combination further reduces the function of the central nervous system, sometimes to the point of coma or the loss of effective breathing (respiratory arrest). This combination can be fatal.

☐ SLEEP MEDICINES
It is likely that non-prescription sleeping medicines, to the degree that they are effective, will lead to the same kind of central nervous system depression when combined with alcohol as the minor tranquilizers (see below).

☐ TRANQUILIZERS—MINOR
(Miltown, Valium, Librium, etc.)
Tranquilizers in combination with alcohol will cause reduced functions of the central nervous system, especially during the first few weeks of drug use. This results in decreased alertness and judgment, and can lead to household and automotive accidents.

☐ VITAMINS
Continuous drinking can keep vitamins from entering the blood stream. However, this situation changes when a person stops drinking.

Index

ABOUT THE AUTHORS

A clinical psychologist, JAMES R. MILAM has been a national authority in the field of addiction for over thirty years. Through his writings and public lectures he has been the leading proponent of the view that addiction is a primary neuropsychological disorder, not a symptom or secondary consequence of psychosocial risk factors, as commonly believed. In addition to many scientific, professional, and public contributions, he has co-founded several model treatment programs, most notably the Lakeside-Milam Recovery Centers in Kirkland, Washington.

As the nation has blindly regressed in recent years into punitive, moralistic attitudes toward substance abuse, Dr. Milam has withdrawn from private practice to intensify his public campaign to present addiction as a highly treatable and preventable disease. His more recent writings are available on the Internet at http://aaw.com. E-mail: drjmilam@ricochet.net.

KATHERINE KETCHAM is the co-author of six nonfiction books, including *Witness for the Defense: The Accused, The Eyewitness and the Expert Who Puts Memory on Trial*, which was a Book-of-the-Month Club selection. Her latest book is *The Spirituality of Imperfection* (with Ernest Kurtz, Bantam). She lives in eastern Washington with her husband and three children.